See page 106
for details

Rs. 35.00

KHUSHWANT SINGH, author and journalist, was educated at Government College, Lahore, St. Stephen's College, Delhi and King's College, London, where he was called to the bar. He shot to literary fame with his award-winning first novel *Train to Pakistan,* and the two volumes *A History of the Sikhs.* Subsequently he edited *The Illustrated Weekly of India* and *The Hindustan Times* with great distinction. Now, as a widely read and syndicated columnist he enjoys the unenviable reputation of "holding a mirror to our face...of being frank, but not venomous, fearless but not intimidating." According to *India Today,* "Khushwant Singh remains perhaps the most spontaneous commentator and raconteur and has provided Indian journalism with some of its most relaxed, tounge-in-cheek writing."

KHUSHWANT SINGH'S JOKE BOOK

Illustrated by Mario Miranda

ORIENT PAPERBACKS

A Division of Vision Books Pvt. Ltd.
New Delhi • Bombay • Hyderabad

ISBN 81-222-0013-3

1st Published 1987
15th Printing 1993
16th Printing 1994
17th Printing 1994
18th Printing 1995
19th Printing 1996
20th Printing 1996
21st Printing 1996
22nd Printing 1997

Khushwant Singh's Joke Book

Cover Design & Inside Illustrations
by Mario Miranda for Vision Studio

Published by
Orient Paperbacks
(A Division of Vision Books Pvt. Ltd.)
Madarsa Road, Kashmere Gate, Delhi-110 006

Printed in India at
Kay Kay Printers, Delhi-110 007

Cover Printed at
Ravindra Printing Press, Delhi-110 006

Preface

In a humourless nation like ours it doesn't take much wit to be regarded as a humorist. It came as a very pleasant surprise to me to discover that the first item most of my readers read in my columns is the last one which I usually reserve for a humorous anecdote. The conclusion is clear: we may not have much humour in ourselves but we enjoy it coming from others. A good joke is a tonic for appetites jaded by an unending and unsavoury diet of politics, corruption religious and social problems.

We take life too seriously and consider far too many topics too sacred to be laughed about. Consequently the little humour we have tends to go on predictable lines. The rustic still enjoys *Boojh Bhujakkar* riddles told by his forefathers; the semi-literates revel in anecdotes about Birbal and Mulla do Piaza. Proverbs and jokes against castes other than one's own being based on stereotypes enjoy perennial popularity: Banias and Marwaris are mean and crafty; weavers are stupid and unmanly; Jats (particularly the Sikh variety) are simple-minded and hot-headed. If you dare to crack caste jokes in the presence of members of the caste concerned, you may well end up with a cracked skull. Sardarjis may tell Sardarji jokes but it would be hazardous for a non-Sardarji to repeat them in the company of Sardarjis he does not know. The people who do not have the capacity to laugh at themselves cannot cultivate a genuine sense of humour.

The humour scene in India has undergone a sea-change since the British and then the Americans flooded our country. They could laugh at everyone right from God and His prophets, the Pope, Kings, Queens and Presidents; down to horses who talked and shaggy dogs who didn't. They were followed by black humour of the Jews and political jokes from countries ruled by dictators; nothing breeds more bawdy jokes than repression. For this we have to thank Stalin, Hitler, Mussolini, Mrs Gandhi's short emergency rule, and General Zia-ul-Haq. Fortunately such jokes are readily transferable from one dictator to another.

I can scarcely take credit for the anecdotes appearing in this book. A large number were sent to me by readers who have been acknowledged by their names. Some others I manufactured or moulded from jokes I picked up from books, magazines and at cocktail parties. My chief contribution in this field is my foolhardiness in publishing them and taking abuse hurled at me. It was not too high a price to pay to take people's minds away from the boring tedium of their daily lives and get them to smile.

Khushwant Singh

For
Prema Subramaniam
My 'Raakhi' sister

A bearded Bengali and a Sardarji got into an argument over which State had produced more freedom fighters—Bengal or Punjab. They decided that for each patriot one named from his State he would be entitled to pluck out a hair from the other's beard. The Bengali opened the offensive with "Khudi Ram Bose" and tweaked a hair from the Sardarji's beard. The Sardarji responded with "Bhagat Singh" and plucked one out of the Bengali's beard. And so it went on painfully with Bengali evidently having an endless list of Bengali nationalists up his sleeve. The Sardarji came to the end of his list. Then with great gusto he yelled "Jalianwala Bagh" and yanked the Bengali's beard off his chin.

Contributed by Harjeet Kaur

An English Colonel of an Indian Regiment once told me that he had been very concerned over fights that frequently erupted between Sikh soldiers serving under him. He made a record of the incidents and discovered that it was usually on Sundays and other off-days when there was no drill, parade or other training to keep them occupied that trouble broke out. So he decided that on every off-day Sikh soldiers should be made to carry their full pack on their backs and made to run round the parade ground for one hour before being allowed off. The trick worked. The soldiers were too exhausted to fight with each other and holidays passed off peacefully.

At a cattle fair there were a large number of prized cows and buffaloes for sale. A man desirous of buying a good buffalo approached a farmer who had a pair of fine-looking animals. The buyer could not make up his mind which one to buy; so he asked the owner the price of one as he patted it on the rump.

"This one will be Rs 5,000," replied the owner. "She is young, will calve every year and is guaranteed to yield 10 kilos of creamy milk every day."

The price seemed a bit on the higher side, so the would-be purchaser patted the other beast and asked: "How much for this one?"

"This will be Rs 10,000. She is middle-aged, has never borne a calf, nor ever will. Her udders remain untouched by human hands."

Flabbergasted with the reply, the purchaser demanded: "What kind of cattle-dealer are you? For a barren buffalo you ask double the price of one that yields."

Janaab, character bhee to koi cheez hai (Sir, there is such a thing as good character)!

Contributed by Prem Khanna, New Delhi

Two men met in heaven. "What did you die of?" asked the one.

"I died of extreme cold. And what about you?"

"I came home from work and heard my wife talking to a stranger. On entering the house, I searched every nook and corner of the house but could not find anyone anywhere. I felt so guilty of my behaviour that my heart failed."

On this, the other one said, "Had you cared to open the fridge, neither of us would have died."

Contributed by M.M. Kapoor, New Delhi

10

A Punjabi couple were always having bitter quarrels with each other. One day a Sardarji neighbour who was a friend of the husband came to reason with his friend's wife: *"Bhainji,* look at us. My Sardarni and I never quarrel because right from the beginning we agreed to divide our responsibilities for all times to come. I make the important decisions and my Sardarni looks after the details."

"But how do you decide what is important and what is detail?" asked the neighbour's wife.

"Simple! my Sardarni decides what schools our children go to, what doctor to send for when anyone is ill, where we take our summer vacations, what kind of car we should buy. And that sort of thing. These are matters of detail."

"And what are the important issues you decide?"

"I concern myself with the Punjab problem, our peace-keeping force in Sri Lanka, Afghanistan, the Middle East and the Star Wars programme."

A deputation of government servants met the Prime Minister and related their woes of stagnating in their jobs. The Prime Minister heard them patiently as is his wont and replied calmly, "I don't mind being the Prime Minister all my life without asking for even one single promotion. I don't understand why can't you be content with being LDCs, UDCs or Assistants."

Contributed by R.B. Kaplish, New Delhi

11

Hashim Ali, vice-chancellor of the Aligarh Muslim University, had his audience in splits when he told the following anecdote:

A vice-chancellor died and was received at the gates of paradise for questioning before his fate could be decided. "What were you doing when living?" asked Dharamraj.

"I was vice-chancellor of a university."

"That's okay. You've suffered the pangs of hell on earth and deserve a break in paradise."

The next arrival was put through the same questioning. "I was vice-chancellor of a university for three successive terms, " he replied.

"Put him in hell, " ordered Dharamraj. "He's got into the habit."

God and Satan got into an argument over the repairs of the wall dividing heaven and hell. God insisted that all the damage was caused by people in hell and Satan should pay for its repair. Satan was adamant that they should share the cost. When they failed to resolve their dispute, Satan said: "Let's appoint an arbitrator and let our lawyers argue the case before him".

"I don't mind having an arbitrator", replied God, "but you will have an advantage over me. I have no lawyers in heaven; they are all on your side".

Contributed by Suddha Basu, New Delhi

This one is also related to the anecdote· of the dispute between God and Satan over sharing the cost of repairs to the wall dividing heaven and hell. When God was unable to find any lawyers in heaven, Satan asked him: "Why don't you argue your own case?"

God agreed to do so. This time Satan was in deep trouble: although all the lawyers were in hell, none of them would agree to take up the brief against God, Satan asked God to agree to an adjournment of the case till Ram Jethmalani arrived on the scene.

"That may take many years, " replied God. "And he may also refuse to argue against me."Being a generous God, He suggested "Why not send him a message and ask him if he will be willing to take up your case?" Satan agreed and sent a messenger to Ram Jethmalani's chamber. Jethmalani felt very flattered. "I feel very honoured that God should have taken my name, " he said. "But I hope to live many more years. If it is an urgent matter, you should hire another lawyer." Just as Satan's messenger was about to leave, Jethmalani had second thoughts on turning down the brief. "Just a minute, " he said to the messenger. "Come to think of it, I will take up your boss's case. There's not much fun left here as the highest in the land does not have the elementary courtesy of answering even one of the hundreds of questions I put to him. It has become a dog's life."

Contributed by Tek Chand Sehgal, Vrindaban

An American delegation on a visit to India were being shown round the capital. In the evening they were taken to the Secretariat for a panoramic view of Vijay Chowk and Rajpath. Came the closing hour and thousands upon thousands of clerks poured out of their offices. The place was crammed with bicycles and pedestrians.

"Who are all these people?" asked the leader of the American delegation.

"They are the common people of India; the real rulers of the country," proudly replied the Minister conducting the visitors.

A few minutes later came a fleet of flag-bearing limousines escorted by pilots on motorcycles followed by jeeps full of armed policemen. "And who are these?" asked the American.

"These are us," replied the minister with the same pride, "the servants of the people."

A Hindu family living in a village near the Indo-Pak border which was often visited by Khalistani terrorists, decided to migrate to another Indian state. Their Sikh neighbours came to bid them a tearful farewell. One of them noticed the head of the Hindu family put in the picture of Sant Jarnail Singh Bhindranwale in his trunk. "Why are you taking Bhindranwale's picture with you?" he asked. The Hindu replied with tears in his eyes, "Whenever I miss my *vatan* (birthplace) I will look at it and feel how lucky I am to have got away."

An elderly and rich *bania* but mean in money matters acquired a young, pretty wife who was a spendthrift. He thought of a scheme to teach his wife the habit of saving. He presented her with a small tin box with a slit in its lid, locked it and put the key in his pocket. *"Meyree Jaan"* he said to her, "every time you let me kiss you, I will put a four anna piece into the box through this slit on top. At the end of the month I will unlock it. All the money in it will be yours to spend as you like".

The scheme worked very well. The young wife showed more willingness to be kissed and her elderly husband was quite happy to part with four anna coins for what he got in return.

At the end of the month with a grand gesture he produced the key from his pocket and unlocked the box. What he saw did not please him because there were many 50 paise and rupee coins in the box. "Where did these come from?" he demanded angrily. "I've only been putting in *chavannis.*"

"Not everyone is as mean as you," replied the wife saucily.

Yahya Khan, trying to persuade a yokel to volunteer for the Pakistani Air Force, took him inside the aircraft and explained: "You press this yellow button and the engine will start. Then you press the red one and the plane will fly off. It is all very simple."

"But how do I bring it down?" asked the yokel, puzzled.

"You don't have to bother about that," explained Yahya Khan. "Leave that to the Indian Air Force."

Vietnamese girls were the GIs' top favourites during American military presence in Vietnam war. "They can be poor in history, but really great on dates," Leo Shaw assures us in his book entitled Confucius Say. Don't be misled by their being bow-legged: "Just because their legs are like ice-tongs, does not mean they are frigid." Their being poorly endowed on the way of busts became the GIs' favourite joke. "As one falsie said to another let's pack up and leave her flat."

Next to getting venereal disease it was having a pregnant girl on his hands that was the GIs' nightmare. The pill was not known and abortions risky. Hence the description of an optimist in Vietnam was one who rubbed vanishing cream on his girl friend's tummy hoping it would disappear. The sanest advice this American Confucius could give the randy GI was, "Women over forty best; they don't yell, don't tell, don't swell and are grateful as hell."

"They say Pakistanis are prospecting for oil in Sindh and Punjab. Is that true?" "Yes. But not to get petrol to run motor cars. Only grease for palms of politicians and ministers."

A gentleman travelled all the way from Islamabad to Karachi to have an aching tooth taken out. The Karachi dentist asked him, "Surely you have dentists in Islamabad! You did not have to come all this way to have your teeth attended to."

"We have no choice. In Islamabad we are not allowed to open our mouths," replied the man with the aching tooth.

An American tourist to India hired a Sardarji guide to take him around Delhi and Agra. When taken to Red Fort at Agra, he admired the architecture and asked how many years it took to build. The Sardarji replied, "20 years." The American remarked, "You Indians are a lazy lot. In America, this could have been built in five years." At the Taj he again admired its beauty and asked how many years it took to build. The Sardarji reduced the period considerably and replied, "Only ten years, sir." The American retorted: "Didn't I say you Indians are slow workers! In America, we can construct such buildings in two-and-a-half years." Same story everywhere. He admired the architecture but reduced the period to ¼th. The Sardarji got irritated. When the taxi was nearing Qutab Minar, the American asked: "What is that tower?" Came the reply, "Sir, I'll have to go and find out. When I was passing this way last evening, there was nothing there."

Contributed by Vijay Gakkhar

A man was taking his four-year-old son for a stroll in the park. They came across an enormously fat man with a protruding belly. *"Papa, yeh kaun hai?* (who is he?), demanded the child.

Beta, yeh udyogpati hai, (son, he is a big industrialist)."

A little later they came across a pregnant lady. The youngster wanted to show off that he had properly imbibed the earlier lesson. *"Papa, yeh bhee udyogpati hai?"*

"No *Beta,"* replied the father, *"Yeh pati-udyog hai."* (Translate that for yourself).

Contributed by Mahendra Kumar Rekhi, Rourkela.

A tiny tot sought admission to the junior branch of a school on the strength of having an elder brother in the final year class in the same school. The elder brother had described the aspirant as his "real brother". When the little fellow appeared before the interview board and was questioned about the relationship, he replied, "he is a distant relative." "How come you call him a distant relative when he says you are his real brother?" asked the Principal. "Sir, there are nine brothers and sisters between him and me, So he has become a distant relative."

The broilers and eggs of a poultry breeder were the best in the market. A man complimented him and asked: "What do you feed your birds to get such excellent products?"

"The very best food: almonds, pistachios, pure ghee mixed in the chicken feed," answered the proud breeder.

"How interesting!" replied the other. "I am from the income tax department. I'd like to know where you got all the money to buy such expensive diet."

Thereafter the breeder was on guard. When the next visitor complimented him on his produce and asked "What do you give your birds to eat?" He replied "nothing, nothing at all. I starve them."

"That calls for action," replied the visitor. "I am from the Society for the Prevention of Cruelty to Animals. I charge you with the offence of starving chickens."

When a third visitor came and made similar inquiries, the breeder was more cautious in his reply: "I give them 50 paise each everyday and let them buy what they like to eat."

Indian VIPs on the hit list have been sent an elaborate set of don'ts to elude terrorists on their trail. Of these the most important are not to follow a regular routine but vary their timings and change their habitat as often as possible, e.g., don't go for your morning or evening walk at the same time to the same park, don't go to the same hotel or restaurant everyday etc. To these precautions, a wit who knows the habits of Indian politicians added: "Don't sleep in the same bed with the same person every night."

A fourth son was born in the home of a minister's family. The father invited his Sardarji friend to join the celebration and choose a name for the new born child. "What names have you given to the three elder boys?" asked the Sardarji.

"One is Rahmat Elahi—(by God's kindness), the second Barkat Elahi (by God's grace) and the third Mahbub Elahi (beloved of God)," replied the proud father.

The Sardarji pondered over the names for a while and replied, "I suggest you name your fourth son, Bas Kar Elahi (God, that is enough)."

Contributed by Mr Hadi of Chittagong, Bangladesh

A couple hired a new chauffeur. The Memsahib asked him to take her out for shopping and was very shaken by the experience. Back home she pleaded with her husband; "Please dear, you must sack this new chauffeur at once. He is so rash he nearly killed me three times this morning."

"Darling, don't be so hasty," replied the husband, "give him another chance."

A grey-bearded Sardarji was asked how his family was doing. "Nothing to complain", he replied stroking his long beard. "Akaal Purukh (God) has been very good to us. I have three sons. The eldest is a *Vakeel*, the second is a doctor, the third a lecturer in a college"

"That is very good. And Sardar Sahib, you must be enjoying your days of retirement."

"No retirement *shitirement* for me," protested the grey-beard. "I ply my taxi, How else could I manage to support my sons and their families?"

I got talking to a Sardarji taxi driver. After we had exchanged information about our *picchha* (village background) he asked me what I did and what I earned. I told him I worked for the Birlas. (I was then editor of *The Hindustan Times)* but did not divulge my salary. Unabashed he remarked: "If I was Birla I would be richer than Birla."

"*Acchaji!* Tell me how you would do that?" I asked him somewhat sarcastically.

Replied the Sardarji: "I would have all Birla's money and also ply my taxi."

This happened when I met Dev Anand. His chauffeur had gone off to get a bite. We sat in the lobby of Oberoi Sheraton to await his return. Clusters of people collected at a respectable distance to gaze at their idol. All I could hear was a hum of "Dev Anands". Then someone asked somewhat loudly: "Who is the Sardar with him."

And someone replied: "Don't know. Must be one of his *chamchas.*"

There is a sizeable corpus of anecodotes about General Cariappa's Hindustani. Starting with his first speech to the jawans on Independence Day "*Aaj ham sab muft ho gayaa*"(today we can all be had for free) to his famous admonition to a road-side urinator (untranslatable and unprintable), they are valuable additions to Indo-Anglian humour based on faulty knowledge of our *bhasha*. What Professor Spooner's juxtaposition of words contributed to English humour, Cariappa's *faux pas* have done for Angrezi-Hindi. To Cariappana I add a new anecdote narrated to me by General Jagjit Singh Arora of Bangladesh fame. It comes from Cariappa's younger days when he was a colonel . At a wedding reception given to a fellow officer, a Pathan and his bride, Colonel Cariappa strode up to the blushing bride , shook her by the hand and asked her whether she had enjoyed her *shahad ka chaand*—honey of the moon.

A Haryanavi peasant was walking down the road carrying a heavy sack of grain on his head. A kindly Sardar farmer drawing his bullock-cart offered him a lift. The Haryanavi gratefully accepted the offer and sat down in the cart but kept the sack on his head.

"Chaudhury, why don't you put down the sack in the *gadda?*"

"Sardarji," replied the Haryanavi, "your cart is already heavily loaded. I don't want to put more burden on your poor bullock."

A rich lady had a family of four children all of whom turned out to be very bright. She was always boasting of their records at school and was sure when they grew up would bring credit to India. I asked her somewhat sarcastically if she had ever heard of the family planning slogan *hum do hamaarey do*. "Yes," she replied somewhat haughtily, "that is for the *aira ghaira-hoi polloi*-not for people like us who have highly intelligent children and can afford to give them the best of education."

"In that case why don't you have five more and give India another *nau ratans*-nine gems?"

She ignored my sarcasm and replied: "I have just read a book on population statistics. It says that every fifth child born in the world is a Chinese."

It is the gossip room of both Houses of Parliament where besides tearing up reputations of politicians, some good anecdotes are manufactured. This one is about Babu Jagjivan Ram's reactions to the new cabinet of ministers appointed by Rajiv Gandhi.

Question: "Babuji, do you think new ministers like K.R. Narayanan and Natwar Singh who have spent most of their years in foreign countries or in aircooled offices in the secretariat know enough about the countryside to be effective?"

Answer: "No, I think they should spend some time in India's villages to get to know villagers' problems."

Question: "In that case don't you think Mr Rajiv Gandhi should also spend some time acquainting himself with villagers' problems?"

Answer: "No, he does not need to do so. He is well-acquainted with them. He knows the Asiad Village."

When Sir Bertrand Glancy was Governor of the Punjab and nearing retirement, Sir Stafford Cripps, who was staying with him at Government House, tried to pull his leg about the very different standard of living he would soon have to get used to in England. Cripps' comment was, "Well, Glancy, you'll have to black your own boots when you get home." Sir Glancy, without a flicker of a smile, replied, "Oh no! I'm going to Kenya where I can boot my own blacks."

It is said that a team of researchers on the sexual habits of city-dwellers interviewed a cross section of Bombay's business community. Among the questions posed to them, one was: What do you do immediately after you have had sex? The answers were most revealing. Ten per cent replied that they simply went to sleep. Another 10 per cent replied that they washed themselves and took some nourishment—a glass of fruit juice, aerated water or a sandwich. The remaining 80 per cent, after much cajoling, replied: "Then we go home."

A lady with five boisterous children boarded a train at midnight at a midway station. The children were very excited and kept shouting loudly disturbing the sleep of other passengers. One of them rebuked the children and angrily told them to shut up. The mother immediately took up cudgels on behalf of her progeny and roundly told the passenger to mind his own business. The passenger settled his score with the lady: "You talk to me in the tone you use when talking to your husband."

A swankily dressed and opinionated young man got into a noisy, crowded bus. With a very superior air he remarked to the conductor: "You seem to have collected all the animals from the zoo in your bus." A passenger retorted, "Sir, not all of them were in the bus till you came. A donkey was missing."

A Hindu, a Muslim and a Sikh were discussing the marvellous achievements of their own brands of surgery. Said the Hindu, "I know of a *vaidji* who joined a severed arm with the use of Ayurvedic glue. You can't even tell where the arm had been cut." Not to be outdone, the Muslim spoke: "A *hakeem sahib* has evolved a new kind of adhesive ointment. He used it on a fellow who had his head cut off. You can't tell where the neck was severed." It was the Sardarji's turn to extol the latest developments in Sikh surgery. "We have gone much further," said the Sardarji thumping his chest proudly. "There was this *chacha* of mine who was cut into two round his navel. Our Sikh surgeon immediately slaughtered a goat and joined its rear half to *chacha's* upper half. So we have our *chacha* as well as two litres of milk every day."

"Why is one Punjabi equal to two Bengalis? asks O.P. Bajaj, a Punjabi living in Jabalpur. He answers his own question with irrefutable Punjabi logic. "Nag is a Bengali. Pal is another Bengali. Put Nag and Pal together and you get one Punjabi, Nagpal."

Ha! Ha!

During one of my periodic bouts with *The Times* (London) crossword puzzles, my eye fell on St Valentine message printed alongside. There were six full columns with almost a hundred professions of love in each column. I was disappointed to find what little progress lovers had made in expressing their affection. More than 500 messages said no more than the three words, "I love you," or repeated the old doggerel: "Roses are red, violets are blue, dizzie darling, I love you." A fair proportion could not even do that and exhausted themselves in a series of Xs presumably expressing desire for labial contact. There were many which were totally inane, to wit : *"Hee hee tee hee hee turn tee, did I say I love you?"* And: "Heffalumpus for breakfast, Heffalumpus for tea, Heffalumpus for ever, when this week you marry me." Lots use private language: "Baby bear loves horrid hedgepig."

Indian emigrants have also found entry in England's love letters. One addressed to Shrimati reads: "You sweet *gulabjamun* of my most delectable dreams! If you don't know what to do, lie back and think of your Indian juice," Many languages are used, even Persian: *Ba hazaran Boseh* (with a thousand kisses).

Two very drunk Punjabis were returning home on a bicycle from the *Theka*—local liquor shop. On the way the man on the carrier fell off; the other cycled on. When he got home he found his companion missing and cycled back towards the *Theka* and found his friend sitting calmly in the middle of the road. The cyclist dismounted and asked gently: "You O.K.?" "I am fine," replied the other, "it is a comfortable carrier seat; keep pedalling unless you are tired."

Contributed by R.R. Bajaj, New Delhi

This one comes from the Delhi University campus and is based on the two meanings of the Hindi word *maang* which can mean both demand and the parting between the hair. Students of a girls college took a procession to protest against living conditions in their hostel. They divided themselves in two groups. One shouted *"hamaaree maangey,"* the second lot replied *"pooree karo."* So they went round the campus yelling "give us our demands."

The procession wound its way past a boys college. The cheerleaders shouted: *"Hamaaree maangey."* Before the second batch of girls could reply, the boys shouted back *"sindhoor say bharo"* —(fill them with vermilion powder).

If you don't get the joke, ask a Hindi-knowing friend.

___

Papa, what is the name of the Indian woman to get on top of Everest?", asked a boy, "I have to prepare for my General Knowledge paper."

His father scratched his head and replied: "I am sorry her name escapes me."

"What was the name of the other Indian astronaut who did not go up with Rakesh Sharma?", he asked again.

The father again looked blank and replied: "I don't know." "Then tell me the names of Indians who have won the Nobel Prize."

"Sorry", replied the father. "I can't answer that one either."

Seeing the look of disappointment on his son's face he added: "But you must keep asking questions. If you don't ask, how will you ever learn anything?"

A firm of solicitors in Bombay go under the name of Patel, Patel, Patel and Patel. The office phone rang and the voice at the other end asked:

"May I speak to Mr Patel?"

"Mr Patel is not in his seat."

"In that case can I speak to the other Mr Patel?"

"The other Mr Patel is out of station."

"Then put me on to the third Mr Patel."

"Sorry, the third Mr Patel has gone out for lunch."

"Okay then I will speak to the last Mr Patel."

"Patel speaking."

A patriotic Sardarji saw the Indian Tricolour fluttering in the breeze. He stood at attention and saluted. "Why did you salute that flag?" asked a passer-by. "It has saffron for the Hindus, green for the Muslims and white for all the others. Nothing for the Sikhs."

Prompt came the Sardarji's reply: "And what do you think the *danda* on which the flag flutters represents? Only the Sikhs."

American astronauts landed on the moon only to find Russians awaiting to greet them. They are comparing notes when they see a family of Sikhs strolling along. "When did you people get to the moon?" ask the Yanks and the Ruskis.

"Many years ago," replies the Sardarji blandly. "We came here after the Partition."

Meetha Mal Goel who has a *halwa* business in our locality went to consult advocate Hoshiar Mal on a legal problem. "*Vakeel sahab,* a dog ran into my shop and before I could shoo it away he took a mouthful of halwa from the big plate. I had to throw the rest away. The *halwa* was worth at least Rs. 50. Please tell me if I can recover my money from the owner of the dog." "Most certainly you can," assured the *vakeel sahab.* "The master of the dog is responsible for what his dog does," "That is very good," said Meetha Mal Goel. "Please let me have Rs. 50 as it was your dog that ate my *halwa.*"

A newly appointed Health Minister of a northern State (guess which?) whose knowledge of English was somewhat elementary was on his first official visit to the largest hospital in the Capital. The Director of Medical Services took the Minister round the operating theatres and general wards till they came to the women patients' section. "This, Sir, is the labour ward," explained the director. The Minister stopped in his steps and remarked firmly: "I will not visit this ward. Don't you know we have a Labour Minister in the government? I must not trespass into his domain."

Mr. T.A. Pai, a former Cabinet Minister, when asked to comment on the "no-change" in the style of functioning and the poor performance of the Janata Government, is said to have remarked:"Why should anyone have expected anything better from them? They are only our B team."

A well-dressed gentleman hurrying along the road was stopped by an acquaintance. "My friend," said the accoster, *sotto voce,* "I must draw your attention to the fact that your fly-buttons are undone."

"I know," replied the well-dressed man brushing aside his acquaintance. "I am on my way to the Income-Tax office to make a voluntary disclosure."

A party of American pressmen were granted an interview with Chairman Mao Tse-tung. After having heard the denunciation of the Soviet Union and other imperialist powers, one of the party asked the Chairman: "Sir, what in your opinion would have happened if, instead of John F. Kennedy, Mr Khrushchev had been assassinated?"

Chairman Mao pondered over the question for a while before he replied, "I doubt very much if Aristotle Onassis would have married Mrs Khrushchev."

Tarlochan Singh of Markfed pumps me with the wonderful achievements of his organisation. He thrusts a large parcel of Markfed products on me: canned fruit and vegetables, fruit juices, jams, pickles and the Punjabi manna- *sarson ka saag.* "We are exporting our *saag* all over the world," he states with evident pride. "You try it out when you are in Bombay; there is nothing like it." There is certainly nothing like it: half a tin consumed will produce enough gas in your belly to make you as airbrone like a jet plane.

A Sardarji is lying across the rail tracks with a bottle of whisky and a tandoori chicken within reach. A passer-by asks: "Sardarji why are you lying on the rail lines? A train may come any moment and run over you."

"Precisely!" answers the Sardarji. "I have no desire to live any longer. I want to kill myself."

"Then why have you this bottle of liquor and the tandoori chicken beside you?"

"Why not?" demands the Sardarji. "You can't rely on trains running on time any more. You don't expect me to die of hunger and thirst, do you?"

This happened during British Raj. The then Sub-Collector of Penugonda (now in Andhra Pradesh) and his "Mem Sahib" were always quarelling. One night the "Burra Sahib" became very angry with his wife and called," You bloody bitch! I will slice you into two": At that precise moment a drunken gentleman who was passing by the bungalow shouted "Please let me have the bottom half."

Contributed by S.N.K. Naidu, Sidhout

A Mrs D. Thomas of Guwahati put in an advertisement in *The Assam Tribune* of 17 July 1985 for the sale of her cottage, land and a pair of oxen. It is not known whether it was the lady or the compositor of the paper who was responsible for the ad that ultimately appeared prominently boxed. It reads as follows: "For sale. Five *bighas* of high land adjacent to N.H. 37, 20 km from Guwahati city on the way to Sonapur, with a small cottage, electricity, deep tubewell with electric pump, cowshed and a pain of bullach."

Contributed by Reeton Ganguly

President Zia-ul-Haq's trusted barber seemed to have become infected by the popular demand for the restoration of democracy. One morning while clipping the President's hair he asked: *"Gareeb pur war!* when are you going to have elections in Pakistan?"

The President ignored the question with the contempt it deserved from a military dictator. At the next hair-cutting session, the barber asked: *"Aali jah!* isn't it time you redeemed your promise to have elections?"

The President controlled his temper and remained silent.

On the third hair-clipping session the barber again blurted out: *"Banda Nawaz,* the *awam* (common people) are clamouring for elections, when will you order them?"

The President could not contain himself anymore and exploded: *"Gaddar!* I will have you taught a lesson you will never forget". And ordered his minions to take away the barber and give him ten lashes on his buttocks.

The barber fell at the great man's feet and whined: *"Zill-i-Ilahi* (shadow of God) I eat your salt; how can I become a *gaddar* (traitor)? I only mentioned elections to make my job easier."

"What do you mean?" demanded Zia-ul-Haq.

"Every time I utter the word election, You Excellency's hair stands on edge and is much easier to clip."

Dr. S.K. Kulshrestha teaching in D.A.V. College, Dehradun, has sent me two examples of the language communication gap which he encountered. Since Dehradun is not far from the Punjab, many Punjabis seek admission to his college. However, since preference is given to UP boys and girls, outsiders are asked to state their "length of residence in UP," and attach their certificates. A boy from a Punjab village filled in his form and against the column "length of residence" wrote, "366 kilometres."

Another applicant filling details of his name, address etc. put against the column "born" the simple reply: "Yes."

The commanding officer got to know that jawans of his regiment were in the habit of giving nick-names to their senior officers. He was curious to know what they called him behind his back. He summoned a young subaltern and questioned him. After some hesitation, the youngster replied, "Sir, they call you virgin."

The commanding officer was pleased. "No doubt it is because of my maiden, innovative ideas I have introduced in army discipline," he said.

"No, Sir," replied the subaltern, "It is because they think you have no experience of any kind."

Contributed by Colonel Beecha

A greenhorn not familiar with the manners of the city folk happened to be spending his holidays with his uncle in Lucknow. During his stay, there was a death in the neighbouring house. The uncle decided to take along his nephew to the bereaved family to offer his condolences. In proper Lucknavi style the uncle began to extol the virtues of the dead man: "He was a great soul. He was not only your *chachaji* but the *chachaji* of our entire *mohalla.* May his soul rest in peace! We will miss him as long as we live." And so on. Our greenhorn maintained a stiff-lipped silence.

Back home, the uncle reprimanded his nephew. "Don't they teach you manners at home? You should also have said something about the dead man being like your own real *chachaji.*"

The lad apologised saying he had never been to condolence meetings with anyone but would bear the advice in mind.

A few weeks later a friend of the greenhorn lost his wife and he decided to offer his condolences in the formula prescribed. "She was a great soul. She was not only your wife, but the wife of all of us in our *mohalla.*"

Contributed by K.R. Prithvi Raj,Matunga, Bombay

Whenever the lady of the house does not want to answer a call (telephone) her bearer replies as instructed, that she is busy answering another call (Nature's). That may be a legitimate lie to use at home but there are limits to the number of times a working memsahib can avail of this excuse during office hours. "Three daily lavatory breaks are sufficient," opines a male employer, "if they seek to go more than four times a day, they should get a medical certificate."

The late Bhulabhai Desai was renowned for his ready wit which helped him to score over his adversaries in debate. Less is known of an equally witty and resourceful person, Sir N.N. Sarkar who happened to be the law minister before Independence. Sarkar was introducing a bill to make provisions for the care of illegitimate children and mistresses who were left unprovided by men they had lived with. Desai thought he would put Sarkar on the spot by asking: "May I know from the Hon'ble law minister what is his government's attitude towards men keeping mistresses?"

N.N. Sarkar was quick to retort: "Sir, we have no first-hand experience of such relationships and will be happy to receive guidance from honourable members like yourself who have more knowledge and experience of the subject."

Since the army is gradually taking over more and more functions of the police, there is much heartburning in police circles. A constable who could not take the reduction of his status much longer, got talking to a jawan: "Bhai, I am told that you jawans of the army have to spend many years on the borders before you get home leave. Meanwhile, your wives go on bearing children. Is this really true? How do you treat these readymade children planted on you?"

The jawan replied coolly: "I do not think this is a common occurrence. But when it takes place we enrol these ready-made children, as you call them, into the police."

Contributed by Tushar, Najibabad

Not to be outdone by Rakesh Sharma and Ravish Malhotra, two sturdy Punjabis applied to NASA, the American Space agency, to be taken to outer space. Their application was accepted and they were asked to report at the centre in California. They were told that during their period of training they must not take any alcohol. They followed the strict regimen imposed on them for several weeks, till one day they could not resist the temptation to wet lips. Since no strong drink was available anywhere near their centre, they drank up a *canister* of rocket fuel. Next morning the following dialogue took place between them: "This is your friend speaking. Have you been to the lavatory this morning?"

"No, why do you ask such a silly question?"

"If you haven't, don't try. I am speaking from Tokyo."

Contributed by Tushar Kumar

Two Punjabi peasants got into an argument over which is more important to the world: the Sun or the Moon. They put the problem to their village *panchayat*. The elders deliberated over the question for many hours before the *sarpanch* pronounced in favour of the moon in sound Punjabi logic:

"If there was no moon we would not be able to see anything at night. The sun shines only during the day when we need no light."

I am beholden to Ganga Saran Sinha for the following two anecdotes of Maulana Mohammed Ali, renowned nationalist leader and a great wit of his times. Ganga Babu assures me their veracity.

The Maulana went to see how the Central Assembly functioned and got a pass to the visitors' gallery. At the time the Presiding Officer was Vithal Bhai Patel. No sooner he saw the Maulana enter the visitors' box, he stood up and announced to the members of the legislature: "It is not customary for the presiding officer to take notice of any person, how ever eminent, in the visitors' gallery. However, I will break all conventions and say how honoured we are with the presence of Maulana Mohammed Ali. I hope it will not be long before we see him as an elected member in our midst rather than seated up in the visitors' gallery."

The announcement was greeted with applause. The Maulana who had propagated the boycott of legislatures under British rule gracefully acknowledged the clapping with a bow and replied: "I am much honoured by your reference to me but would prefer to stay where I am so that I can look down on all of you".

On another occasion the Maulana who had received a doctorate from Al Azhar University of Cairo decided to visit the Central Hall of Parliament in the *Chogha* (gown) presented to him. It happened to look very much lika a *burqa* and combined with the Maulana's flowing locks gave him a somewhat feminine appearance from the rear. In those times the Central Hall was equipped with a bar where drinks were available at very cheap rates. A member somewhat high with liquor decided to have crack at the Maulana. "For a moment I thought we had the pleasure of Begum Sahiba's company in our midst. From the rear you look exactly like a woman."

"I am sorry to disappoint you", retorted the Maulana, "my wife would never agree to come to an assemblage of *hijdas.* I don't have any such inhibitions."

A certain gentleman from Northern India built a house without a roof. When asked why he had not completed the job, he replied: "Don't you know that the Government has decided to put a ceiling on all urban property?"

Professor K. Seshadri of Jawaharlal Nehru University has stumbled on the origin of the word *chamcha.* It was believed that it might have been derived from the spoon-shaped shoehorn with which an orderly helped his sahib to put on his boots. Now he has come across a far more plausible explanation in the diary of Freidrich Engels in which the communist philosopher records the visit of Queen Victoria to Cologne. The mayor of the city, a commoner with notions of grandeur, had his daughter serve the Empress a cup of tea. The Empress haughtily took a sip from a spoon and turned her back on the girl. Engels writes: "The poor girl stood trembling awfully, not knowing whether to stand or to go away. Served her right! These purse-proud bourgeoise, with all their cunning are with their worship of kings and queens but spoons afterall, and as such deserve to be so treated."

Three young women, a Tamilian, a Maharashtrian and a Punjaban who happened to die the same day arrived in the office of Dharamraj, the keeper of life's records. He first questioned the Tamilian about her life-style. "I have been very good; a virgin till I married, utterly faithful and dutiful to my husband. I looked after my mother-in-law and prayed to Tirupati everyday."

"That's very good. I will recommend you for first-class accommodation in Paradise," said Dharamraj.

The Maharashtrian came next. "I was a full-blooded Maratha so I could not be quite as chaste in thought and deed as my Tamilian sister. But I didn't hurt anyone and I kept my husband happy."

"For you second class accommodation in Paradise," replied Dharamraj.

"And what about you?" he asked the lady from the land of the Five Rivers.

"I was a very bad woman," she replied. "I did everything I shouldn't have done; I never said my prayers, I quarrelled with my *saas,* and had an affair with my *devar* (husband's younger brother)."

"That was very bad, *behenjee,"* said Dharamraj.

"Do anything you like with me but don't call me your *behen,"* snapped the Punjaban.

"Okay! In that case you come to my apartment this evening."

Wives of two members of Parliament were comparing notes on their husbands. Said one very proudly: "My husband can talk all day long on any subject you think of."

Not to be outdone, the second lady replied: "My husband can do better. He does not need a subject and yet he can talk and talk and talk."

This anecdote travelled from Poland, where martial law has been lifted, to Pakistan where it is still in force. A Pakistani soldier was caught trespassing in the private quarter of a home. The house-owner hauled him out into the street and both he and his son began to thrash him. A passer-by joined them. The military police rescued the soldier and arrested the three men. They were arraigned before a military court.

"Assaulting a man in military uniform is a very serious crime punishable with death," said the presiding officer to the three accused. "What explanations have you to offer as extenuating circumstances."

The elderly houseowner replied: "Sir, I caught this man trying to molest my daughter. The honour of a Pakistani daughter is more sacred than one's life."

"Quite right!" agreed the presiding officer. "And what do you have to say?" he asked the houseowner's son.

"Sir, this fellow was trying to take liberties with my sister. The honour of a Pakistani sister is more precious than one's life," he replied.

"Quite right!" agreed the presiding officer and turned to the third accused. "You are not related to these people; you did not even know who they were? Why did you join in the assault?"

"*Ghareeb parwar*—defender of the poor—forgive me. I made a terrible mistake. When I saw these two men beat up this fellow in uniform, I thought martial law had been lifted. So I thought I could also settle my scores with the army."

We are six men at the dinner table. The others are from Somalia, Saudi Arabia, Kuwait, Tunisia and Morocco—all five Muslims. The first course on the menu is lobster. The Somalian shakes his head, examines the card, and seeing what is to follow, askes the waiter to get him a plate of chicken. He sees his fellow Muslims eating lobster and admonishes them in Arabic. I catch the word *zabah* (slaughter) bandied between them and gather that the Somalian is telling them that since shell-fish like lobsters cannot be slain in the manner prescribed by Islamic law, it would not be eaten by Muslims. The next course is pork. The Somalian shakes his head again and repeats his request for chicken. Being amongst Muslims I also say "No" to pork and opt for chicken. The other four accept it and fall to it with relish. More angry words are exchanged between them. I catch the words *khanzeer* (pig) and *haraam* (unlawful). The Somalian tells me that his fellow Muslims feel that dietary laws of Islam do not apply when they are not in Muslim lands. The waiter arrives with flasks of red and white wine. The Somalian asks for coke; the rest of us have our glasses filled with juices of fermented grape. And once more argument breaks out. While they are at it, the waiter places plates of chicken in front of the Somalian and myself. The Tunisian turns the tables against the Somalian by asking the waiter "How did you kill this chicken you serve my friend? Did you recite the *Bismillah* when you slit its throat and let it bleed to death?"

The waiter who is a Buddhist does not understand. The Somalian looks very unhappy. "Let me eat my chicken in peace," he protests. They reply: "You let us enjoy our meal and we will let you enjoy yours."

The Dutchman-turned-American, Peter de Vries, a reputed writer asks himself; "What does humour deal with besides that which isn't funny? Bad food, undertakers, broken machinery, husbands, wives, brats. It is the Aristotelian principle you laugh at that which, if there were more of it, it would be painful. Humour deals with that portion of our suffering which is exempt from tragedy."

Vries has more wit than humour. To wit "We are all like the cleaning woman. We come to dust." "It is clever but not very funny." The same goes for his epigrams: "The blood donor makes up for the hit and run driver;" or somebody "who like the condemned man refused to order a big last meal because he did not want to put on more weight;" "celibacy is the worst form of self-abuse." His puns are just about okay, e.g.:

"Ever since I unlisted my telephone number, I have been getting more crank calls."

Vries' witticisms are not my idea of what jokes should be. They should have more kick in them than there is in an epigram, a pun or a turn of phrase. And a joke must not demand too 'much thinking from the reader, Like P.G. Wodehouse, "I like to keep my jokes as limpid as dammit."

Question: What is common between the Indo-Pak border and postal envelopes issued by the Indian Post Office?

Answer: Neither can be sealed.

Contributed by Kamaljit Singh Ahluwalia, Amritsar

At an international seminar on the study of Crustacea one section was devoted to crabs from different parts of the world. Separate species were put in large glass jars with muslin covers to prevent them from clambering up and escaping. However, the jars containing Indian varieties were left uncovered. Visitors noticed this strange phenomenon and asked the curator in charge why Indian specimens had no muslin tops to prevent escape.

"You see, these are Indian crabs." he explained, "No sooner one starts going up another of its own species will immediately claw it back. There is no danger of anyone getting too high up."

I am not sure of the precise meaning of the word gay. Does it apply to males who are exclusively homosexual? Or does it include men who normally consort with women but occasionally deviate and have sexual relations with other men? If the latter, then a sizable proportions of celebrities could be described as gays. Shakespeare's sonnets reveal his passion for a boy. Sultan Mahmud's love for his slave, Ayyaaz, is as celebrated an example of consuming passion in Urdu poetry as that of Majnoon for Laila. Mughal Emperors, despite their well-stocked *harems,* confessed to lusting after boys. I had read of Babar's crude comparisons of parts of the male anatomy to water melons but had not realised that his son, Humayun, inherited the same trait till I chanced upon a couplet composed by him:
I saw a Hindu boy arrayed in battle,
His face was flushed as if with wine,
"Your ruby-red lips bewitch me, 'said, I
"Humayun, they are not made of stone, was his reply.

A number of well-wishers who called to condole with me when my mother died said they had come "to condone" my mother's death. Ma, forgive them for they did not know what they said! They meant well. As did my photographer friend T.S. Nagarajan, who, whenever he wanted to say he did something with deliberation would say "I wantonly did." There was never anything wanton about Nagarajan; he is as strait-laced a Tamil as I know.

Philip Norman of *The Times* (London) has new crop of malapropisms which I had not heard of before. He writes of his grandmother's verbal gaffes. After visiting her sister in hospital she described the "sirloin" drip attached to the patient's arm with doctor's "hoovering" around and giving her "the R.I.P. treatment".

Another lady working in a haunted house had to call in a priest to circumcise" (exorcise) the ghost. In a restaurant the excellence of the food served was ascribed to the chef who had earned a *"Condom Bleu"*. (Cordon Bleu or the blue ribbon awarded to the best of cooks).

Malapropisms did not end with Mrs Malaprop's description of a person being "as headstrong as an allegory (alligator) on the banks of the Nile." They continue to be as many splendoured as "all the colours of the rectum" (spectrum). Heard of any new ones?

Question: What is the difference between members of the Dal Khalsa and members of the Hindu Suraksha Sangathan?

Answer: One have Khalistan in in their heads; the others have *Khalli* (empty) *sthaan* (space) in theirs.

This comes from a young entrant to the Indian Administrative Service. His first posting was a junior assistant to the Secretary of the Ministry. One morning he took some important files to discuss with his boss. After knocking on the door and receiving no reply, he gently pushed open the door to find his senior standing by the window deeply engrossed in his thoughts. He tip-toed out of the room. Since the files were marked "immediate", he went back to the Secretary's room and, again receiving no reply to the knock, went in. The boss was still standing where he had been and intently looking out of the window. Junior Sahib coughed lightly to make his presence known. The Secretary turned round and remarked, "How can this country go forward! For the last one hour I have been watching the workmen on the road. They haven't done a stroke of work."

A man went upto heaven to complain to the Good Lord about the sorry state of affairs in the world. "Almighty God, you are said to be all-knowing. I don't think you know a thing about what is going on the earth that you created. No one cares a fig for the truth."

The Almighty Lord protested: "I know exactly how things are down below. Look at that board in front of you. Everytime anyone tells a lie, a red light flashes and I know who is lying."

The man watched the flicker of red lights on the board and was duly impressed. Suddenly a whole lot of red-lights began to flicker madly. The man asked, "Why are all those lights flickering at once?"

Replied the Almighty—"Oh that! we are tuned into All India Radio & Doordarshan."

This anecdote is about two Indians settled in England. One had been living there for some years and had caught on the some of their quaint euphemisms. The other, a recent settler, was as yet unaware of them. They were invited for dinner by their English friends. After they had their drinks, their hostess asked them, "Would you like a wash before I serve dinner?" The knowledgeable one replied, "No thanks." The new settler replied, "I washed my hands before I came."

On their way back after dinner the older settler admonished his friend. "My dear chap, in England 'would you like a wash' does not mean 'would you like to wash your hands.' It is a polite way of asking would you like to urinate?" The new settler made a mental note of it. Some days later when he was invited by another English friend and after he had his drinks he was asked by his hostess: "Would you like a wash before I serve dinner?" He replied promptly, "No, thank you madam. I washed against a tree before coming to your house."

When the young boy of family passed his school leaving examination with flying colours, their next door neighbour came in to felicitate him. "Consolations! he burst out with great enthusiasm. "You worked very hard; preservance (perseverance) always pays."

More visitors came to offer their congratulations. Many were strangers to each other. So one of them took upon himself to introduce them: *"Aaiye main aap ko insay* intercourse *karva doon,"* he said. This needs no translation.

Contributed by S. Deb, New Delhi.

I reproduce the following excerpts of Churchill's wit sent in by Samiran Sarkar because I had never heard of them.

Sir William Joyson Hicks made some statement in Parliament to which Winston gave signs of demurring. "I see my right honourable friend shakes his head," said Hicks, "but I am only expressing my own opinion." "And I," answered Winston "am only shaking my own head."

The genuineness of Churchill's joke about Sir Alfred Bossom's entry into the House has never been questioned. "Bossom?", he said, "What an extraordinary name....neither one thing nor the other."

Once when his race horse Colonist II finished fourth Churchill had his own excuse. He said that he had a serious talk with the horse just before the race. "I told him this is a very big race and if you win it you will never have to run again. You will spend the rest of your life in agreeable female company."

Then Churchill added, "Colonist II did not keep his mind on the race."

When a General during the Second World War pompously asserted that "putting the troops in the picture before a battle was the sort of familiarity which breeds contempt", Churchill retorted: "You know General without a certain amount of familiarity it is extraordinarily difficult to breed anything at all."

Churchill's grandmother, the Duchess of Marlborough, had this to say on the arrival of her grandson:

"I have myself given birth to quite a number of infants. They were all pretty vocal when they arrived, but such an earth shaking noise as this newborn baby made I have never heard."

An elderly Punjabi admitted to the intensive care department of a hospital made a request that he should be allowed to take lessons in Urdu. The doctor in charge was very puzzled and asked him the reason why. "Urdu is the language of angels," replied the Punjabi, "if I die I want to be able to converse with all the *houris* I will meet in Paradise."

"How can you be sure you will go to heaven?", asked the doctor, "You may go down to hell, then what good will Urdu, you call the language of angels, be to you?"

"That will be no problem. I am fluent in Punjabi."

K.N.P. Rao from Bangalore has sent me an amusing piece illustrating how the communication gap may yield dividends. In Santa Monica, California, one of the late Swami Muktananda's Indian disciples runs a flourishing Siddha Yoga centre. The *Ashram* is spread over three motels in which his disciples are housed. A dispute arose over whether the motels were to be assessed as business premises or exempted from tax as parts of a religious institution. The locals supported the Swamiji. When the Swamiji who speaks very little English went to thank them, they replied they wanted him to stay because of the business he brought them. The next thing the Swamiji did was to buy dozens of bullet-proof vests and give them away as gifts to Santa Monicans. "Well", said their spokesman apologetically, "the Swami speaks a combination of Hindi dialects that few can understand. So when we told him we had a vested interest in having him stay, I guess he took us literally.

Many Santa Monicans strut about wearing bullet-proof vests.

India's refusal to participate in any game in which South Africa is represented provoked a writer to try and hurt India on what he believed would be its most sensitive spot—the practice of untouchability. How many untouchables had played in India's Test teams? he asked. The Chairman of the Indian Cricket Board replied: "It is not clear to me what you mean by asking me to send the information regarding untouchables who had played representative cricket for India. If by the word 'untouchable' you mean any Indian player who has participated in South Africa, I have to inform you that there is no Indian player who can be called an untouchable."

When I read the slogan "Give an MP a good night out", I was filled with envy of English Parliamentarians. When I read further "Today, several London MPs will be offered a good time by 110 fetching young women" *(The Times)*, I was peeved. Why can't some comely Shrimatis launch a similar project beginning with giving Indian MPs resident in Delhi "a good night out"? As always happens with dreams of dalliance, there was a rude awakening. The fetching young English women are after money and what they offer in return is no more than their company at an opera or a ballet and thereby persuade them to vote against the cuts proposed by the government in the art's budget. If any of their guests gets wrong notions about what their lady companions meant by giving them a good night out, they will be told gently that the name of the organisation is Society of London Arts Publicists. If the full name does not enter the thick skull of the MP and his hand strays to where it should not, there is the short, sharp acronym: Slap.

Most of it was punning on words. An absolute nugget is a repartee between poets Urfi and Faizi, court poets of Emperor Akbar. The *takhallus* "Urfi' means well-known. Faizi's father's name was *"Mubarak"* meaning auspicious. One day when Urfi paid a visit to Faizi he found the latter playing with his pet puppy dog. "What is the name of this young master?" asked Urfi.

"I call him Urfi", replied Faizi, "because he is well known".

"Mubarak baashad! most auspicious choice," retorted Urfi.

I have received an unsigned letter from a lady from Batala. She asked me to reply. She writes: "For unmarried women beyond 35 years, who do not wish to marry or live with anyone but wish to have children—the way to artificial insemination is the only possible solution. I do not care at all about the society or its views. But I do wish to raise my voice in favour of this solution. Why should unmarried women suffer lack of children when modern technology is offering such a solution? I am in the middle of this complex problem myself."

I reply: Dear Madam, thanks for the opening. Your knowledge of the process of conception seems somewhat limited. Artificial insemination is not *the only* possible way of conceiving without being saddled with a husband. There is a much pleasanter way of achieving the same object. If you need further elucidation, please drop by for personal consultation. No fee will be charged. Privacy will be assured. Yours faithfully—K.S.

S.K. Singh , our Ambassador in Islamabad, has a gift of putting everyone at his ease. During a recent visit to Delhi he happened to call upon some friends who have a precocious five-year-old daughter. After having exchanged pleasantries with his friends, S.K. felt he ought to talk to their daughter. In his most charming diplomatic manner he asked the child:

"Beta, what school do you go to?"
The child told him.
"And what are your favourite subjects?"

The child ratteld off her favourite subjects.

More question followed; and answers given. S.K. thought he had done his duty as a guest. The child decided it was her turn to ask questions.

"And uncle what do you do for a living?"

"I am an Ambassador. Beta do you know what an Ambassador is?"

The child nodded her head wisely and replied: "Yes, Daddy has one."

A Punjabi matron emigrated to England taking her only son with her. She took to the country like a duck to water. But her boy missed his village and began to waste away. Ultimately the lady took the boy to the local doctor for a medical check-up.

"Does the boy eat well and sleep well?" asked the medico.

The lady replied in her Punjabi English: "*Na, na doctor sahib, Na eatda, na saleepda; but weepda hee weepda.*"

Contributed by H.S. Rattan

V.K. Krishna Menon was a bachelor and hated people with large broods of children. In his early career as a barrister, a neighbour couple with three girls in toe called on him and suggested that he accompany them to a theatre as they had an extra ticket. The sixsome waited for a bus and the first one had only room for four (No overloading.) The second one came after five minutes and had only 3 vacancies and the third had two. So they decided to walk the distance instead of being late for the show.

Menon with his walking stick was tramping on the cobble stones on the pavement and tuck-tuck-tucking. The father, already irritated with not getting the bus, remarked, "Dammit, Krishna, can't you put a piece of rubber at the end of your stick?"

Pat came the reply: "If you had put one at the end of yours, we would have got into a bus.

Contributed by K.S. Menon, Bombay

A man went in a bar and ordered a drink. After he had lushed and got up to leave. The bartender asked, "What about the bill?"

"I have already paid", he replied and left.

Soon after, another man came in. He, too, ordered a drink, drank it and left saying that he had already paid.

The third customer came in. As he was drinking, the bartender told him, "Before you two men came here, they ordered drinks and left, telling me that they had already paid. What do you think about that?"

"Stop arguing and return my change," the man said.

Contributed by Ajay Sood, Delhi

A student of Munich University has been placed first inventing a machine that does absolutely nothing useful. The contraption picks up slips of paper from a file, passes the sheets through different levels, stamps them, crumples them up and throws them into a waste-paper basket. We Indians can take the credit for having invented such machines over half a century ago; they can be seen in action in all our government departments. The German has patented his invention under the name Ministerium. Readers are invited to suggest appropriate names for the Swadeshi product. I promise to send the winner my latest paperback collection of essays—unless he says, "No, thank you."

A middle-aged couple got into a crowded Delhi bus. The husband gallantly gave the one free seat to his wife and found himself behind a well-stacked college girl. He took advantage of every jerk and turn to impress his person on the lass' posterior. The girl did not want to create a scene and kept quiet. His wife also suffered the spectacle in silence. As fate would have it, all three disembarked at the same stop. And no sooner were they out of the bus, the girl turned round and gave the man a tight slap across his face, "How dare you pinch my bottom? You should be ashamed of yourself," she screamed.

"But, but, but", muttered the man. "I did not pinch your bottom."

"No, he did not," intervened the wife. "I did. I saw what he was doing and wanted you to teach him a lesson, *Dhanyavaad."*

53

The executive Committee of the club of which I have been a member for the last 40 years decided to raise its annual subscription. In due course followed a circular telling members that henceforth they would have to pay so much per annum. Whether it was the secretary's poor knowledge of Latin or the printers, one of the ns in annum was missing. A member wrote back to enquire why this new mode of paying subscriptions had been authorised: "In the past we have been paying through our noses, why is payment now demanded through our posteriors?" he asked.

Kakey da Hotel is a very popular eating-place in Connaught Circus. It started off as a humble *Kakey da Dhaaba* with stools and *charpaees* laid out on the pavement and the *tandoor, handees* and *pateelas* placed in the open. With prosperity the kitchen went into the rear and a dining room was furnished with tables, chairs as well as wash basin. One evening a patron having finished his meal went to rinse his mouth in the wash basin. He proceeded to do so with great vigour; gargling, spitting *thooh thooh* and blowing his nose. This ruined the appetites of other diners who protested to the proprietor. Kakaji went to the rinser-spitter and admonished him. "Haven't you ever eaten in a good hotel before?", he demanded.

"Indeed, I have", replied the errant mouth-rinser, "I have eaten at the Taj, Maurya, Oberoi, Imperial, Hyatt."

"What did they say to/you when you rinsed your mouth making all these unpleasant sounds?"

"They asked: 'You think this is *Kakey da Hotel?*' And threw me out."

Kakey da dhaaba has evoked another anecdote on cheap eating places. An Indian abroad ran out of foreign exchange and went looking for the cheapest eating place in town. He located an Indian restaurant and went in. He found three sections: "European, Chinese, Indian." He went into the Indian. It was divided into two: vegetarian and non-vegetarian. He went into the vegetarian which was further sub-divided into pure ghee and vanaspati. He went to the Vanaspati section and found yet another division: cash and credit. Cheered at the prospect of not having to pay in foreign exchange he opted for the credit section. When he got to it he found the sign: "exit: get out."

A Sardarji and a Bengali were travelling in the same railway compartment. It was very hot and the Bengali was having trouble undoing the steel strap of his wrist-watch. The Sardar went across and with one might jerk undid the buckle. "You Bengalis should eat *gehoon* (wheat). It makes you strong."

The Bengali did not appreciate the advice. A few minutes later he grasped the alarm-chain and pretended to be unable to pull it. Once again the Sardarji leapt to his assistance and pulled down the chain with a triumphant yell: "There! You Bengalis should eat..."

The train came to a halt. The conductor accompanied by a couple of policemen asked the Sardarji to explain why he had pulled the chain, and on his failure to do so, fined him Rs. 50.

After they had left, the Bengali gently advised the Sardarji, "You Punjabis should eat rice. It is better for the brain."

This Khalistani anecdote has been sent to me by Kanwaljit Kaur and Manohar Bhatia. A Khalistan Roadways bus plying between the state's major towns had a Nihang conductor. "Where to?" he asked a young Sikh passenger before issuing him a ticket. "Amritsar", replied the youngster. The Nihang conductor gave him a clout on the head and said, "It is Sri Amritsarji Sahib". The youngster quickly corrected himself, "Yes, of course! One for Sri Amritsarji Sahib." The next passenger was a Hindu. "Where to?" asked the Nihang. "Sri Ludhianaji Sahib," replied the other timidly. He too was rewarded with a clout on the head. "Only Ludhiana, no Sri or Sahibji," admonished the Nihang before issuing him a ticket. The third passenger happended to be a wordly-wise Marwari. When asked for his destination, he replied: "Nihangji, kindly give me a ticket for Sri Amritsarji Sahib; thereafter I will go on foot to my village." the Nihang was pleased: "If you are not completing your journey by this bus, no need for a ticket-*shiket,*" replied the Nihang.

I owe this true anecdote about Pandit Nehru to Jagan Nath Kaushal, our Law Minister. In the good old days when things were cheaper and MPs less grabbing, their salaries were fixed at Rs 400 per month. To this figure, Nehru as P.M. added another Rs 20 as monthly allowance. Somebody drew his attention to the fact that the total 420 was capable of uncharitable comment. Apparently at that time Nehru had forgotten the little he knew of Section 420 of the Indian Penal Code which defines cheating. He was quick to grasp the innuendo and promptly raised the total figure to Rs 421.

General Zia driving round Islamabad came across long queues of Pakistanis outside several embassies wanting visas and entry permits to go abroad. He got out of his car and joined a line to find out why so many people were wanting to leave the country. No sooner did people see their President with them they left the queue to return to their homes. President Zia asked them why they were doing so. They replied: "If you are leaving Pakistan there is no need for us to go."

Two readers, Kanwaljit Kaur and Manohar Bhatia, have sent in what are claimed to be true anecdotes from the anti-Sikh riots in Delhi. A reporter visiting a slum area saw a man throw out of his jhuggi a roll of expensive terricot fabric. When asked the reason why, the man replied, "I looted it for my family but not no one likes the colour; it is too dull." At another slum colony he saw a man smashing up a TV set. When asked why, the fellow replied, "I wanted a colour TV: this is black and white. I have one of that kind with me already."

I came across this charming little doggerel during my brief sojourn in Hong Kong recently:
Please don't send me to the hospital
I know what will happen.
Hospital will grab my purse,
Switch me from nurse to nurse,
I'll go from bed to worse;
And end up in a hearse.

Deccani Hindustani is a constant source of amusement for northerners. Whenever I happen to be in the erstwhile domains of His Exalted Highness the Nizam I try to veer the conversation round to make them say *hao* instead of *haan* (yes) or *nakko* instead of *naheen* (no). The words sound sweet when mouthed by young *puttas* (male urchins) or *puttees* (female urchins). The other day I was in Hyderabad's Patthar Gatti bazar looking for Urdu publications. The going was very *halloo halloo* (slow) because of the chaotic tangle of cycles, cars, tongas and flocks of black-burqa ladies going to Latha Bazar to buy lac-n-glass bangles. I stopped beside a *dargah* beneath the Char Minar where a fellow was lustily blowing through his shehnai hoping to drown other noises of the city. I heard a lot of *hao's* and *nakko's* and asked my escort for an explanation. He told me of an anecdote of a Lucknawi gentleman who on a visit to Hyderabad had like me wanted to know the reason. A highly literate Hyderabadi friend replied: *"Janaab-i-wala,* educated Andhras always say *Jee Haan* for yes sir, it is only the illiterate who say *hao."*

"You always say *Jee haan,* you must be highly educated"

"Hao"

Children's favourite dirty jokes have more to do with breaking wind, defecation and human bottoms. But, concludes Jill Tweedie, they are revolting enough to turn the stomachs of adults. Truly the grown-up is more in need of protection from the infant pornographer than the other way round. Another instance of the child being the father of the man, what?

Mughal Emperors were sticklers about court etiquette. Places were assigned to courtiers according to rank and none besides princes of royal blood allowed a seat. When ordered to approach the throne, the first step forward had to be taken with the right foot and the person had to stop at a prescribed distance from the monarch. Even close relatives had to observe these rules.

Badauni records a transgression of etiquette by the daughty Bairam Khan who was the seniormost of courtiers while attending on Humayun. The Emperor was being longwinded in his speech and the aged courtier who was overcome with drowsiness became inattentive. Humayun spoke sharply "Bairam Khan! we are speaking to you and you seem not to be listening to us."

The old man roused himself and replied "Yes, your Majesty, I am all ears. I am told that in the service of Kings, watch should be kept over the eyes; among *dervishes* watch should be kept over the heart; and among men of learning, watch should be kept over the tongue. Your servant was wondering what he should keep a watch on as your Majesty is at once a King, a *dervish* and a man of learning."

I scan the "death" columns of most daily papers. 'But for the grace of God', I say to myself, "I would be seeing my own name in print." Could any reader enlighten me why Punjabis "leave for their heavenly abode", Bengalis "pass on", and all other Indians simply "expire"?

59

In the last year of his service a certain Babuji was made head of the cash section. All vouchers had to have his signatures before they could be cashed. He introduced a new system whereby his prior approval was required in writing before any purchases could be made. It worked so well that he decided to introduce the same system in his home.

One Sunday his wife sent him a note saying that the children wanted to eat pakoras; hence a sum of Rs. 15 may kindly be sanctioned for purchasing oil, besan, paalak, etc. The husband recorded that oil and besan had become too costly and beyond the reach of a middle-class family like theirs; hence the proposal was rejected.

Next Sunday his wife sent another note saying that she wanted to accompany her friends to a movie; hence an amount of Rs.20 be kindly sanctioned for a cinema ticket and refreshments. The husband recorded that the pay of a government employee is almost finished by the 20th of the month and it being the last Sunday of the month, there was no money left with him. The proposal may be re-submitted in the first week of the next month. The wife got irritated and wrote an application saying that she had not visited her parents for long and should, therefore, be granted leave for one month. The husband wrote, "Leave granted, Substitute may be arranged."

Contributed by R.R. Bajaj, New Delhi

Question: "What did the little boy tell his father when the radiator of their new Maruti-Suzuki developed a leak?"

Answer: *"Maruti nay Soo Soo Kee."*

Shri O.S. Bhatnagar from Mathura sents us a portion left out of the complaint made by the hapless passenger, whose ablutions resulted in his missing his train.

"While me fall down in hurry to ride the going train I was saw the dam guard shouting the whisle and moving the flag (which contry it was I didn't now), but he keep standing on the platefarum not try enter to the compartment. Was he go by aeroplan to next stashun?

"Make a juge inquiry and sent the results to bearded Happy Time Lion in his den at Horn Bye Road, Bombay, who passed to me."

One must not be too hard on a poor fellow whose knowledge of a foreign language is elementary. Much funnier are linguistic *faux pas* committed by those who assume familiarity with a lingo without really knowing it. I recall an angry letter written by a teacher of English to the chairman of her school. "Dear Sir, I wish to resignate..." The sound of words often causes confusion in simple minds. A semi-literate but rich business man intending to make a bequest to a co-educational institution was dissuaded from doing so by one who wanted the money for his own boys' school. "Do you know that in the co-ed school boys and girls share the same curriculum?" he asked the donor. "Moreover they matriculate together." To drive the point home, he added: "And worse than that they spend most of their time in Seminars."

The bequest was never made.

From the number of letters I received, it would appear that linguistic bloomers are a very popular form of humour. Most of us who are anglicised wogs switch from our native languages to English, interspersing each with words from the other. Even the uneducated make free use of English words. I heard a *qawwali* singer complain that, because of her inattentive audience, *"Mood kharab ho gaya."* A labourer reprimanded the foreman: *"Mere kaam mein interfere mat karo."* And I hear the word "bore" in almost all Indian languages.

Then there is the mauling of foreign words. A lady reluctant to give up a seat she had occupied proclaimed: I am not *nickling* from here." Mr Pandu Chintamani of Bombay sends a report conveyed by the guard of a train in which the lights were on the "blink". It read *"Bijlee is bajanging... if any haraj maraj ho gaya, Guard is not jumevar."* I don't believe it. However, here is one of my favourites.

A Minister for Housing (name not disclosed for fear of causing "hatred, ridicule or contempt") was presiding over a committee considering plans for building urinals. The plans were examined and passed. The Honourable Minister made the concluding address: "Gentlemen, now that we have sanctioned plans for the construction of urinals, it is only appropriate that we should take up the scheme for raising arsenals."

Pragati Grover, of Lady Sri Ram College sent me suggestions of gentler ways to keep an over energetic Sardarji occupied and kept out of mischief. One is to give him a piece of paper with P.T.O. written on both sides. If this does not work then put him in a circular room and tell him to look for the corner of the room.

Everything about the Japanese is impressive save their galling inability to learn foreign languages (a Japanese Hullo becomes a Haro) and their queer sense of humour. They take their pleasures very sadly. See them at their Pachinko parlours grimly pouring metal balls in slot machines and you will know what I mean. Their favourite game is to pile matchsticks on the mouth of a bottle. They seldom laugh, but when they have had their quota of Sake (it takes very little to light them up) then they roar. They find a hole in a sock irresistibly funny. Their jokes have a quality of their own. Here is a Jap version of a honeymoon joke.

In the middle of the first night of his honeymoon the bridegroom (married on his 25th birthday) was roused by the telephone: "It's me, your mother. Happy birthday."

"Thank you Mama but why did you have to wake me up at 2 a.m.?"

"Because you did the same to me 25 years ago."

A couple went to a fair. In the milling crowds the two were parted from each other. The husband reported the loss of his wife to the police and advertised it in the newspapers. No trace of the lady could be found. As a last resort the husband went to temple and made a tearful prayer before the image of Sri Ram Chandraji: "Bhagwan! I have lost my wife. Please use your divine powers and restore her to me."

Bhagwan Ram Chandraji replied: "My good man! go along the road till you get to the temple of Hanuman. When I lost my wife, it was Bajrang Bali who found her for me."

A sales agent of firm of tobacco manufacturers was haranguing a crowd of villagers on the benefits of imbibing the weed which assured longevity. "Those who smoke never grow old," he proclaimed. An octogenarian grey-beard in the audience spoke up in support of the tobacco vendor: "Brothers, he is quite right!" When a young man takes to smoking, he dies by the time he attains middle age. That saves him from old age."

An Indian peasant who made a vast fortune abroad but acquired nothing besides money was anxious to return home quietly lest his grasping relatives stake their claims to his wealth. A press reporter asked him as he was about to embark on his homeward flight: "Sir, are you going back *incognito*?"

"No," replied the rich yokel, "I am going back by Air India."

Sir John Greenborough's contribution is about a shy bachelor posted as ambassador to Peru. At a reception and dance given by him in the embassy he spent more time with his whiskey bottle than with his guests. Emboldened by the intake of spirits he decided to ask what appeared to him his most important lady guest, to dance a Viennese waltz with him. The guest turned down the request with the following words: "There are three reasons why I will not dance with you. The first is that you have obviously had too much to drink. The second is that the orchestra is not playing a Viennese waltz—it is playing the Peruvian national anthem. And thirdly, I am the Cardinal Archbishop of Buenos Aires."

My short piece on Indian mispronunciation of English evoked many examples from our readers. One from the South is indignant that I should have lampooned Tamilian accent because "the very best English is spoken in Tamil Nadu. And the worst by the Punjabis. Professor Viswanathan from Mangalore writes about his English teacher's advice that the *"Jorality* of the composition lies in the *dadabudality* in the usage of words." (For the life of me I cannot work out what the learned teacher was trying to say!) He also wrote to say that a Sikh doctor diagnosed some ailment as *"penewmonia."* That sounds a very sick Sikh joke!

A friend living in Japan sent me two examples of linguistic tribulations in foreign lands. A young Sardarji on a bicycle tour of the world was pleasantly surprised to find that at every restaurant he went to people had heard of him and wanted to hear his story. The Sardarji obliged by narrating an account of his travels. The Japanese sibilate their h's; hence the Japanese word Hitori meaning table-for-one-sounded like a request for his story to the Sardarji. Appended to this letter is a true ancedote—not of pronunciation—but of Japanese inscrutability. A Japanese gentleman desiring information on India before embarking on the voyage called at our Tourist Information office on a Ginza.

Japanese: How far is Agra from Delhi?
Information Officer: 120 miles.
Japanese: And how far is Delhi from Agra?
Information Officer: 120 miles.
Japanese: *Wakarimashta! Domoagrigato!*
(I have understood, thank you!)

How does it come about that one word should have different meanings in different regions? Take the example of English as it is spoken in England and as it is spoken in the United States. Across the Atlantic it has become so different as to earn the name of a new language, Amerenglish. Most English words are still recognisable in their transatlantic reincarnation, but not all. There are a few which have assumed embarrassing transformations. The most celebrated of these (and to which I have referred earlier in these columns) is the slang, fanny. In the American edition of Raymond Chandler's *Farewell My Lovely,* Klopstein had spoken of "two warts on a fanny". In the British edition the same reads as "two warts on a behind"- for the simple reason that while fanny is the front of an American female, it is the posterior of the British *memsahib.* A correspondent commenting on the phenomenon writes:

An English Tourist usually finds
That US fannies are behinds
But Anglo-vocab's contrapuntal;
Here fannies are full female frontal.

A much shorter version of the same which swipes at yet another verbal oddity runs:

Across the sea the electric message hums
Assess is donkeys—arses is bums.

For some strange reasons, sexual overtones are much in evidence in the examples quoted in the British Press. Harold Evans, Editor of *Sunday Times,* commenting on the expression "to goose", suggests that it is an Americanism "indicating vigorous digital probing with erotic intention."

In England "to goose and duck" is used for more full-blooded sexual activity without any doubt of the erotic design.

In India too we have the same vocabularic phenomenon. Why should a Dada be a grandfather in

Northern India, a respected elder brother in Bengal but a thug in Maharashtra? Likewise a Kaka is like the French Cadet, the youngest of the siblings in the Punjab, but an uncle elewhere. It would appear that the one relative we are agreed upon unanimously in denigrating is the wife's brother *Sala.*

A Japanese tourist having lost his way in Amritsar approached two constables and asked them the way to the railway station. He first spoke to them in English. They shook their heads and replied: "No English Sapeekk." He took out a pocket book and put the same question in French. The constables again shook their heads. The Japanese took out other books from his haversack and tried out Spanish, German and Russian. His efforts evoked the same negative response from the two constables. After the Japanese left them to seek assistance elsewhere, one constable said to other: "Natha Singha, we should learn some foreign languages. We could be of more help to these tourists."

"What use!", replied Constable Natha Singh emphatically. "This Japanese spoke to us in five different languages. Where did they get him?"

Winston Churchill, when asked for permission to allow 60 MPs to go up on a trial flight of a newly designed aircraft, Winston said a firm no. "I think it would be disastrous if suddenly the country were plunged into sixty by-elections. Besides which, throughout my long public career I have always maintained that it is unwise to put all your *baskets* into one egg."

Correspondent N. Sharma from Ramgarh (Bihar) sends a clipping of a tender for supply of school equipment put out-of all people-by the office of the District Superintendent of Education. It invited "Quotationers" to make offers for the following articles:

1. Bras and Bell-1 kg with wooden humber
2. Jumetry set in wooden box
3. Glob-8″ dymiter
4. Bucket (Balti) 10″
5. Spad Nos of tata
6. Aluminium mfg for one liter
7. Wooden Black Board 1 big 5″ x 3½″ for shakhua wood with two kari
8. Wooden Black Board (Small) 31½″ x 2½″ for shakhua wood with two kari
9. Maps - India world Tirhut Commissionary and West Charaparan Rajnaitik and Historical map of Bihar historical approved by survey department.
10. Charts-Digesting system skelton Health sanitation historical Bhawan Kala Darshan Shambidhan Jiwa Vigyan Bhawtik Vigyan Rashayan Vigyan.

Now you know why Biharis are amongst the most illiterate in India.

Robert Atkins MP had this dig at Khrushchev. At a public meeting the Soviet leader was denouncing Stalin. Somebody from the audience shouted: "As one of his colleagues at the time, why didn't you stop him?"

There was deathly stillness, Khrushchev thundered "Who said that?" There was no response. After a long and petrified silence Khrushchev replied to his question himself, "Now you know why."

Two men were involved in an angry agrument. One was a burly Sardarji; other a frail Bania. Sardarji who was getting the worst of the argument lost his temper and slapped the Bania.

"Did you hit me in anger or did you do it in *mazaak* (jest)?" demanded the Bania.

"Of course I slapped you in anger," roared the Sardarji.

"That's alright", replied the Bania, "because I don't like to be made *mazaak* of."

Lahore's *Viewpoint* had a column recently by someone called " U No Who" condemning such "nauseating things as a young thing in tight blue jeans devouring a hot dog at Kalloo the Kababee". He writes:

"I am not joking. Pakistan was not created for such things as hot dogs and hot pants. About hot pants and the Mulla, I have an interesting story which I shall tell you later, but first things first. Imagine what it would mean if we go national and translate into Urdu this thing, these hot dogs - *'garma garam kutte' Tauba! Tauba!*....

And now the Mulla. He walked into a ready-mades store and asked for "hot pants".

"The manager corrected him: 'You say woollen, not hot.'

" 'Very good, Sir,' said the Mullà.

"Now after all this he wanted a cup of tea and went to a restaurant and called out to the waiter: 'O ye! I want a single very woollen tea...' "

V. J. Nair from Allahabad has sent me the wrapper of what appears to be a kind of bleaching powder. The singular "Direction for use" is reproduced without emendation:

A small quantity of Sunblue Wrape In piece of cloth dip it in the fixed taken water for use of white clothes.

Then maintain the sky blue colour in the water, against it wash white clothes with soap powder. Rinse thoroughly in clean water, dip the clothes one at a time, turn wring and hang to dry.

Proprietors of the bleach may be forgiven: A *dhobi* does not have to know English to wash your clothes. But you would expect better from a brochure of a film. The opening paragraph of Kala Chitra's film *Free Love* runs as follows:

Love is bondage—It was now-a-day's it is free. This is the age of Free Love or at least that is what today's youth think—Let us presume it is Free. That means any hand can have access to any wasit—and that Loving hand can slowly reach the neck the Finish, Death.

Epitaph-Collecting is my favourite hobby. I have quite a few witty farewells to life in my repertoire. *Two Monsoons* by Theon Wilkinson, who indulged in the same ghoulish pastime, has added two gems to my collection.

A soldier drowned in the Chenab has this on his tombstone; "Out of the depths have I cried unto Thee, O Lord". Another one in Peshawar runs: "Here lies Captain Ernest Bloomfield, accidentally shot by his orderly, March 2nd, 1879. 'Well done, thou good and faithful servant' "

71

An anti-Establishment joke: A vagrant, finding no place on the pavement, parked himself at the feet of a statue of Mahatma Gandhi. At midnight he was wakened up by someone gently tapping him with his stick. It was the, Mahatma himself. "You Indians have been unfair to me," complained the benign spirit. "You put my statues everywhere that show me standing or walking. My feet are very tired. Why can't I have a horse like the one Shivaji has? Surely, I did as much for the nation as he! And you still call me your Bapu."

Next morning the vagrant went round calling on the Ministers. At long last he persuaded one to join him for a night long vigil at the feet of the Mahatma's statue. Lo and behold, as the iron tongue of the neighbouring police station gong struck the hour midnight, the Mahatma emerged from his statue to converse with the vagrant. He repeated his complaint of having to stand or walk and his request to be provided a mount like the Chhatrapati's.

"Bapu," replied the vagrant, "I am too poor to buy you a horse, but I have brought this Minister of Government for you. He...."

Bapu looked at the Minister and remarked: "I asked for a horse, not a donkey."

Sharmila Tagore rings up the Wankhede Stadium and asks for her husband. "Madam, the Nawab Sahib has just gone in to bat," says the voice at the other end. "Can I take a message or will you ring up later?"

"I'll hang on," replies the film-star Begum Pataudi, "He never takes very long at the wicket."

"There are three ways to bring about social change in India, "said Sarvodaya leader Jayaprakash Narayan. "They are summed up in three Ks: *Kanoon* (law), *Katal* (murder) or *Karma* (deeds)." It would appear that *Kanoon* has failed to deliver the goods and we do not have the energy for *Karma*. Hence the Naxalite third: *Katal*. The moral is quite clear, said Jayaprakashji, who, as a committed pacifist, abhors Naxalite methods. "If we have to avoid violence then we must see that laws are enforced."

Two tigers who had escaped from the Delhi Zoo reappeared in their respective cages after six months of freedom. One was very fat, the other reduced to skin and bone. They began to discuss their experiences. Said the thin one: "I was very unlucky. I found my way into Rajasthan. There was famine. I could not get enough to eat. Even the cattle I killed had no flesh on them. I would have died to hunger, so I decided to surrender myself to the police. Although I am caged here, at least I get my bellyful of meat every day." He asked his fat companion why he had come back to the zoo.

"At first I had very good luck," replied the fat tiger licking his chops in happy reminiscence. "I got into the secretariat. Every evening, as the millions of Babus poured out of their offices, I used to catch one and eat him up. For the first six months no one noticed anything. But yesterday I made the mistake of eating up the fellow who serves them their relays of cups of tea and coffee. Then they let hell loose on me. Take my word, it is safer behind the bars than being at the mercy of those bloodthirsty Babus."

At every presidential election there are many candidates. We get so absorbed in the contest between the top favourites that we tend to overlook the merits of the half a dozen or more worthy gentlemen and often a lady or two who humbly offer themselves as future tenants of Rashtrapati Bhavan. We've heard a great deal about Sanjiva Reddy, Chintaman Deshmukh and V.V. Giri, but how many of us know of Sarvashri Hari Ram, R.K. Mital, Khubai Ram, Ramanlal P. Vyas, Mr Santosh Singh Kachwaha, Mr. I.N. Singh (a 60-year-old Patna kisan) and Shrimati (I beg Her Highness pardon!) Gurcharan Kaur of Nabha! I have received a hand-out entitled "Amongst his many qualifications he would have us know is the following: I am a married man with four children and have undergone vasectomy in 1965. Earn and learn is my motto and that proved immensely helpful in my life."

A celebrated film star (I can't remember whether it was Myrna Loy or someone else but she was one of Hollywood's top actresses at the time) asked to meet Dr. Radhakrishnan to discuss some problem philosophy. I conducted her to Dr. Radhakrishnan's retiring room. He was lying on his bed in his thin muslin dhoti and vest. He pushed away a pile of books and made room for the visitor and asked her to sit beside him. The film star hesitated for a moment before she lowered herself gingerly on the philosopher's bed. He took her hand and asked her: "And, my dear, how many husbands have you had so far?" (At the time the lady was contemplating marriage to the leader of the American delegation.) She opened her heart out to him. No philosophy was discussed.

There was the boss of a firm in Australia where absenteeism was endemic. He spoke to the workmen: "Looking about me I see a number of faces that are not here; what I have to say applies particularly to those who are absent, and I hope they will listen attentively and make a note every word."

A similar story is about a signpost at a road junction. "This way to Timbuktu—if you can't read, enquire at blacksmith's opposite." Then there was a signpost along a creek which read: "When this sign is under water the crossing is dangerous." Some signs have a macabre sense of humour as one leading to a cemetery: "One-way traffic." An exhortation to city dwellers when they come to seek peace and quiet in the mountains: "Keep still and listen to the silence." A number of Aussies follow the instruction and one asks: "I cannot hear anything, can you?"

Bishen Singh Bedi stands in the centre of a market-place tossing a cricket ball and addressing passers-by: *"Behno aur bhaiyo!"* Soon a large crowd collects round him. Bedi continues to toss the cricket ball and yell: "Brothers and sisters!"

A man approaches him and asks: "Sardarji, why don't you say something? See the enormous crowd you have collected."

Replies Bedi: "Sir, you have no doubt seen lots of fools play with different kinds of balls on different kinds of playing fields. But I bet you haven't seen so many fools gather round one cricket ball."

The original story is in untranslatable Punjabi and far too obscene, Try and work it out. It was narrated to me by none other than Bishen Singh Bedi.

Vice-Admiral Lord Mountgarret, while addressing an all-male gathering of sailors where everyone present knew as much about sailing as he, His Lordship who had by then imbided more than his share of spirits decided to talk about his sexual exploits of which he claimed to have had many more than they. The next morning while His Lordship was nursing his hangover in bed, Her Ladyship ran into one of the previous evening's audience while she was out shopping and asked him how her husband's speech had gone down. "He was roaring success," the man assured her.

"I am so glad," said Lady Mountgarret. "I was terribly worried. He's only done it three times. The first time he was violently sick. The second time his hat blew off, and the third time he got all tangled up in the sheets!"

It is a great pity our legislators lose their tempers so readily. Much more can be achieved by ready wit than by angry demonstration, yelling slogans, abuse, fisticuffs or walk-outs. I recall an encounter between the late Feroze Gandhi and a senior Cabinet Minister given to acid remarks about everyone and with an exaggerated notion of his own ability. This minister was said to have described Feroze Gandhi as the "Prime Minister's lap-dog." Then he had the misfortune of getting involved in a financial scandal. Feroze Gandhi was scheduled to open the debate in the Lok Sabha. He is said to have walked up to the Minister and within the hearing of the Treasury benches said: "Mr So-and-So, I hear you have been describing me as 'a lap-dog. You no doubt consider yourself a pillar of the state. Today I will do to you what a dog usually does to a pillar."

Once I gave an example of a repartee in the Lok Sabha. I have just stumbled on a perfect gem—of all places from what must be one of the smallest democracies in the world, Uruguay. An angry Senator was attacking a Minister of Government. The Minister tried to interrupt the Senator's speech. "I haven't finished yet," roared the Senator, and went on in his near-defamatory tirade. Each time the Minister tried to protest, the Senator yelled, "I haven't finished yet," At long last when the speech ended, the Minister asked, "Have you finished now?"

"Yes," replied the Senator taking his seat.

"Then pull the chain."

The man a sour spinster had hoped to espouse had married her best friend instead and then risen to great eminence. When I asked the jilted lady how she felt about the fellow, she replied with a serpentine hiss: "You know what! I would have liked to be that man's widow.

I never heard Siddheshwari Devi sing but know a few anecdotes about her. When she was invited to England she was eager to make her mark at her first concert scheduled for a select audience of European connoisseurs of oriental classical music. She failed to tick. When asked why she was off colour, she remarked, "When I looked at the audience I could not get it out of my mind that these people wiped their bottoms with paper and their tails were dirty." Nice tail piece what!

Galbraith is a very gifted reconteur. He once told me of the experiences of an American couple who came with an introduction to "Mr Singh of Delhi". Their friends had assured them, "You cannot miss him. He wears a turban and a beard and drives a cab." The poor couple had the misfortune of running into a Mr Singh who answered to the description and proceeded to take the Americans for a ride. (The Americans' naivete has to be experienced to be believed!) Mr Singh presented them with a bill for Rs.400 for two days of sight-seeing. By then they had noticed that most of the city's cabs were plied by men with turbans and beards—and almost all of them answered to the name Singh.

Galbraith's favourite after-dinner anecdote was about his visit to Bengal. A very enthusiastic officer from the department of agriculture was appointed to escort him on a tour of the countryside. The young man went on endlessly about plans, projects, hydro-electric power, afforestation, compost pits, etc. In order to show some interest in his surroundings Galbraith pointed to a clump of eucalyptus trees and asked, "Are they indigenous?"

"Oh yes, Sir, they are very indigenous," replied the agriculture expert. "We got them from Australia."

A hero of World War I was approached by a young girl and asked: ;"Did you kill a German?" The hero replied in the affirmative. "With which hand did you do it?" demanded the girl. "With this right hand." The girl took the hand and kissed it. An officer who was watching the proceedigs exploded: "Heavens, man, why didn't you tell her that you bit to death?"

Two IRA men were driving to the location where they intended to plant a time-bomb which one of them had in his lap. "Drive a little slower—this bomb may go off any minute," said the man carrying the explosive. "Don't worry, assured the driver, "We've got a spare one in the boot."

I owe this follow-up on the making of a minister to Dr. I.C. Dawoodbhoy of Bombay.

"The son was expected from abroad after a five-year jaunt. The father invited his best friend to his house on the day of arrival and took him to a room where the son was to be shown in. He pointed to the four things he had placed on the table. If he picks up the money, he said, he will be a businessman. If he takes the Bible, he will be a pious, religious man, if the bottle of liquor, he will be a drunkard and a waster and if he picks up the gun, he is going to be a gangster. Both of them waited behind the curtain and watched. As the son walked in, he noticed the four items on the table. He opened the bottle of whisky and took a long swig; he pocketed the wad of currency, put the gun in his hip pocket and the Bible under his arm and calmly walked away. "Dammit," said the father, "he is going to be a Minister."

An editor of one of the hundreds of journals that mushroom every year was in the habit of visiting business houses to seek advertisements. If the ad was granted he would carry it with a picture of the owner of the business house captioned with glowing tributed to his "qualities of head and heart". If it was not, he would write somethings scurrilous about the owner of his family or his products.

One of his regular advertisers was an aerated drinks factory. After many insertions, the firms decided to call a halt because the publication had a very small circulation. The next issue of the journal carried in banner headlines how consumption of that brand of aerated water caused impotence, sterility and other kinds of diseases. The editor also had posters printed and plastered on the walls of the city to make sure that the message got to the masses. It did. The sales of the fizzy concoction declined. When the owner realised that there was little he could do and going to the law would land him in endless and expensive litigation, he simply left the town and asked his manager to handle the situation.

The manager wrote a very friendly letter to the editor inviting him to the office to talk things over. The editor walked into the trap. He arrived expecting to contract for a year's advertisement. He was welcomed, shown into a room. And thoroughly beaten up. Before he got to the police station to lodge his report, the firm's lackey had registered a complaint of trespass and assault, displaying torn shirts and bruises on their bodies. The editor found himself in the lock-up.

An American tourist arrives in India; it is his first visit to the country. He hires a cab for the day to take him round the city. Outside a bakery, he espies a big mob jostling, pushing, everyone trying to get in at the same time. "What is going on?" he asks the Sikh taxi driver.

The Sardarji is very patriotic and does not wish the foreigner to have an unfavourable impression of his country. "They are shooting a film," he replies blandly.

A little later they come to a yet greater mob of people outside a ration shop selling wheat and cooking oil. Jostling, pushing, everyone trying to get in at the same time. "What's going on here?" demands the American.

"It's the same film; part second," replies the Sardarji and drives on.

A third mob outside the kerosene oil depot. Men, women and children banging their tin cans, raising a hell of a shinding. "And what's going on here?" asks the visitor.

"Same film; part three," replied the Sardarji.

"Say, what kind of film is this? What's it called?" demands the Americans tourist.

'It's a documentary of India," replies the Sardarji. "In Hindustani it is called *Sattaee Saal baad*."

I asked an Amritsari if there was a red-light area in the city. "No," he said. "Fortunately, there is no prostitution in Punjab since 1947." I expressed disbelief: What do your errant young men and the rich do for their pleasure:" He replied, "They go to Delhi or Bombay."

81

My own encounter with racial prejudice is a mild brush with a drunk at Heidelberg station. I do not understand what he says but the tone is offensive. I insist that my escort translate for me. "He thinks you are some kind of Turk and wants to know why you carry that shit bag on your head," interprets my escort, very embarrassed. I laugh and say: "Tell that *dreckschweine* (filthy pig—a term they often use for Turks) I am not a Turk but a Hindu (all Indians are Hindus) and that what I have on my head is a turban." The escort does not oblige.

The drunk has caught the word *dreckschweine* and decided to follow me to the waiting room. I sit there for some time listening to him ranting away. A policeman comes along, apologises to me and takes the fellow away.

On arrival at Frankfurt I am met by my escort—a young and not unattractive girl who has just acquired a doctorate in philosophy. I make a beeline for the newsstand to get English papers while she pushes my luggage in a trolley. I hear Punjabi voices and turn to look back. There are half a dozen boys eyeing me and the German *fraulein*. As we go ahead to the taxi stand I hear one of the boys remark enviously: *"Yaar, buddhey ne to phuta-phut kabootri phasa li."* (It has not taken the old man much time to trap a dove.)

Nijalingappa arrives at the Prime Minister's house to escort her to a meeting of the Congress Working Committee. "Indiraji, are you Reddy?" he asks.

"No," replies our lady Prime Minister, *"Main giri"* (I fell down).

But she was more than ready for Reddy.

I had always used the expression WOG, to refer to people like myself, the brown sahibs. And believed it as an acronym for Westernised Oriental Gentleman used to describe Europeanised Egyptian gentry. The etymology is now disputed. It came to light following the speech made by Sir Richard Dobson, head of British Leyland, to what he believed was a private gathering. His hosts' son came armed with a secret tape-recorder and passed the tape on the Tariq Ali who sold it to some papers. Dobson had to resign for using this offensive expression for coloured people.

Now a lively controversy on the origin of WOG has started in the British Press. It is agreed that it was born in Egypt to denote workers on Government service engaged in the construction of Suez Canal. "My 700,000 colleagues and I in the civil service are, of course, WOGS," claims one Englishman. "No," writes another Limey (Englishman) "WOGS in the Near and Middle East called us Giabours" (infidels). Apparently the infidels retaliated by calling the faithful WOGS. "It is not a colour label," insists this correspondent. "It was a nickname applied to cheerful porters at various ports and depots in Egypt handling War Office General Stores (WOGS)."

Willy Brandt, the heart-throb and Germany's Jack Kennedy of yesteryear, faced his downfall in public esteem due to his kowtowing to the Russians, known in Germany as Ostpolitik. A German paper discribing Brandt's meeting with Dubeck, the Czech victim of Russian expansionism, placed him inside the stomach of Comrade Brezhnev. "He ate me up," explained Dubeck. "I came the other way," replied Willy Brandt.

An American research team eager to measure the advances in technology made by different nations devised a thinner-than-human-hair metal wire and took it round the world to see what other nations could do to it. The Japanese proved their skill by boring a hole in it. The researchers arrived in India with the thin-holed wire and challenged our technicians to improve upon it. They were directed to Ludhiana. They were taken to a workshop run by a Sardarji mistri in his backyard. The Sardarji examined the wire and told the researchers to come back an hour later. When the team returned at the appointed hour, he handed them their wire. They could see no change. "Examine it under a magnifying glass," commanded the Sardarji. They did. Printed on the wire was the legend: "Made in India".

Kantibhai Lalloobhai emigrating to Europe by ship happened to share the table with a Frenchman. As they met for the repast the French man bowed and wished him *bon appetit*. Kantibhai, believing the other man was introducing himself responded, "Kantibhai Lalloobhai." So it went on at every meal till a friend told Kantibhai what *bon appetit* meant. The next time he encountered the Frenchman, Kantibhai bowed and said *bon appetit*. The Frenchman responded, "Kantibhai Lalloobhai."

Once upon a time a woman brought her son to the Prophet (on whom be peace) and complained: "O, Messenger of Allah, please do something for this lad. Despite my admonitions he contines to eat dates all the time and boils have erupted on his body." The Prophet (on whose progeny also be peace) asked the lady to see him a month later. When the mother and son came a second time, the Messenger of God simply told the boy to stop eating dates. The lady remonstrated, "O Holy One, if this is all you were going to say, why couldn't you have said it a month ago when we came to seek your guidance?"

The Holy One replied, "Last month I too was eating too many dates which I love. I could not give advice to anyone to stop eating them till I had myself got the better of my addiction to sweets."

The moral has seldom been better told: do not preach to others what you do not practise yourself.

Sardar Swaran Singh, despite his lack-lustre approach to foreign affairs, has undoubtedly delivered the goods more than any of his predecessors. My friend Satindra Singh of the *Economic Times* who is a great raconteur and fabricator of anecdotes told me this after Sardar Swaran Singh's successful encounters with the Pakistanis. According to Satindra, Swaran Singh learnt diplomacy in his village. Across the street lived a young lass who made it a point to display her charms to rustic lads who passed by. She led them on but never yielded to their overtures. "That's what I did," Sardar Sahib is reported to have said, "Give them visions but nothing else."

Once every three months or so an elderly lady who was once prominent in the women's movement calls on me. She brushes aside my secretary, ignores the notice saying "No visitors before 11 a.m. and thereafter only by appointment", opens the door and asks, "Can I see you for a moment?", and without waiting for an answer enters the room. She is well meaning and soft-spoken. I offer her a chair. She takes some time to compose herself by covering her face with her hands and thinking deep thoughts. Then she bares her smiling face and starts the dialogue with the question: "Sardar Saheb, tell me, where is our country going to ?"

I shrug my shoulders and make some helpless noises which imply, "I don't know." She is satisfied and puts her second question :

"What are you doing about it ?" I hold up my hands in a gesture of helpless resignation and reply : "What can I do ?" She tells me what a pleasure it is to discuss national problems with someone as well informed as me and takes her leave.

There was a Pakistani officer who broke into the house of Bangla Professor and saw three pictures on the wall : Kazi Nazrul Islam, Mr Jinnah and Gurudev Tagore. He assumed that Nazrul Islam's photograph was that of a Hindu so he shot it with his revolver. Then he sprang to attention and saluted the portrait of Mr Jinnah. "And who is this fellow with the long hair and beard ?" demanded the officer. "Sir, that is the father of Quaid-e-Azem Jinnah," replied the quick-witted professor. The soldier sprang to attention and saluted the portrait of Tagore.

At a game between India and Russia which I witnessed, while the Indians cheered the Russians when they pulled off good shots, I did not see the Russian visitors (there were over a dozen sitting in the row in front of me) cheer the Indians. At one stage when Metreveli was questioning the verdict of the linesman, the crowd started yelling and booing. An Indian lad who could be no older than ten years of age screamed "No cheating" as he would in an interschool tournament. A Russian sitting in front turned back and snapped angrily, "Watch your words !" The boy promptly apologised. His father was apparently stung by the unnecessary reprimand and bided his chance to retaliate. When Kakulia was having his ankel massaged the boy asked his father, "Daddy, if he is hurt, why doesn't he stop playing ?" "He's afraid of being sent to Siberia."

By evensong we are driving on Delhi's Ring Road: The row of temples along the Jamuna's bank is loud with clanging of bells. Smoke rises from funeral pyres at Nigambodh Ghat. The slums are gone. Instead there are neatly laid out lawns, flower-beds, cunningly placed lights. Delhi gets cleaner and more beautiful every day. I recall Prof. Madhok chiding me for giving credit to everyone except the people who have done it. "It's the Jana Sangh administration that has rid Delhi of its slums, given it parks, dual highways, new schools, colleges, hopitals. You did not have one kind word to say about V.K. Malhotra or any of his colleagues," he had insisted. I concede my bias, "I don't like Jana Sangh politics." The Professor smiled, "If you were not Sikh I would have said that's a Sikh answer." I give in.

At the home of P.M. Rungta, President of the Board of Control for Cricket in India, I met our team on its way to England. Most of the evening was spent hearing reminiscences of the Vice-Captain, Venkataraghavan, and the spin bowler, Bishen Singh Bedi. Venkat has a charming way of telling a joke against himself. At the end of a Test match at Leeds, an Englishman walked up to him and asked if he could have the honour of shaking hands with the Indian player. They shook hands and discussed the match in some detail. Venkat was impressed with the Englishman's knowledge and asked how he knew so much of the game. "I have played a little cricket in my time," replied the Englishman modestly. Venkat thought his face looked familiar and asked his name. "My name is Herbert Sutcliffe," replied the other.

Lady Reading seldom lost her Viceregal poise and attended every function in spite of failing health, but she had her own sense of humour. Sir Conrad Corfield, an ICS officer in India for 22 years, relates the following incident in his book, *The Princely India I Knew*. One evening, when the Viceroy's orchestra was performing during dinner, she enquired the title of the dance tune which was being played. No one could remember. So her A.D.C. was sent to ask the bandmaster.

The conversation at the table changed to another subject during the A.D.C.'s absence. He slipped into his seat on return and waited for an opportunity to impart his information. At the next silence he leant forward to catch Lady ‘Reading's eye and, in a penetrating voice, said, "I will remember your kisses, Your Excellency, when you have forgotten my name."

A firm which undertakes to destroy vermin has sent me its terms of contract. If its ability to kill pests is as great as its ability to kill the English *bhasha* then I can strongly commend it. Instructions are:

1. Before start the work empted every thing.
2. In the bed room cuboards to be empted.
3. When the Job is started, nobody can stay inside after fumigation to keep two hours in the Flat.
4. After open the Flat only clean with dry cloth.

"Is that too, jeero, too, phor, phipe, eight?"

"It is, madam."

"I am tasting you, sir."

You like my taste?"

"Hokay."

A mother narrates a dialogue between Willy Brandt and his assistant in a plane. Said Willy, "If I throw a 100-mark note, it would make at least the one German who found it happy again.'

"Ten 10-mark notes would be a better idea," replied his assistant. "They would make 10 Germans happy."

The pilot who overheard the conversation butted in "If I threw both of you out it would make 50 million Germans happy."

I was chosen to be the guinea pig for Jagjit Singh's first book *Mathematical Ideas*. "If you can understand it," he said complimenting me, "any ass will understand it." So from guinea pig I turned an ass and dutifully brayed my understanding.

There was a period during the Pakistan army's campaign of repression which was directed exclusively at the Hindus. Every Bangla Hindu tried to pass off as a Muslim. The Pakistan army couldn't be fooled that easily. During one of *pogroms* they lined up all the adults of the village. "Name?" asked the officer. "Moosa Mian," replied the man. "Lift on your *tehmad.*" Moosa Mian did as he was told. He was allowed to go. The next one, Hindu, was understandably nervous. "Name?" demanded the officer. "Atul Bihari," replied the man, shaking with fear. "Why are you so scared?" demanded the officer. "We are not looking for Biharis but only Hindus."

A Sardarji lost in the crowd was accosting English-men and asking them for directions in Punjabi. One Mr. Bali went to his rescue and put him on the right bus—which he also happened to be taking. In the course of their conversation it transpired that the Sardarji had been in England for many years. Mr Bali could not help asking: "Why have you not learnt how to speak English?" Wouldn't it be easier for you to earn your living if you could speak their language?" The Sardarji was unabashed. "Why should I? Were these English fellows speaking our language when they were exploit-ing us? When I have enough money, I will go back to my village and live as I used to. No English Phinglish for me!"

And there was a tailor who specialised in making Kurtas known in Bangladesh as punjabis. He was interrogated by the Pakistani CID. "What do you do?" The tailor replied, "Sir, I am a cutter. And what do you cut?" "Sir, I only cut punjabis." He was promptly put under arrest.

Many friends have complained about the treatment they receive from Ministers of Government and their flunkeys (chamchas — feeding spoons). They have been thrown out of circuit houses and dak bungalows. Often a four-berth railway compartment is reserved for the pleasure of one V.I.P. They may take comfort in the reply given by a British Minister of Transport to a request for a list of those entitled to the privilege of a whole railway compartment to themselves.

He replied: "Cabinet Ministers and lunatics; His Majesty's Judges of Assize and verminous persons; and corpses."

In Tokyo I saw a film produced and directed by Mishima. The theme was *Harakiri*. He as the hero disembowelled himself with a Samurai sword. This is exactly how he ended his life sometime later.

I discussed the affair in sombre tones with Naomi Mitchison. "You should carry a series on suicide." she replied. "Start with Mishima. Call the series 'Do It Yourself".

General Tikka Khan of Pakistan and his troops left a sizeable anthology of jokes which are still recounted there. Their pattern is very much the same as those manufactured by Jews under Hitlerite tyranny. My informant was young Himayetuddin of the press Information Directorate who was my escort during my three-day sojourn. Here are a few samples.

A farmer brought his pride rooster to sell in the market, "What do you feed that bird that he is so big?" asked a Pathan soldier of the Pakistan army. "I feed it rice, Sir," replied the farmer. "How dare you waste rice on the bird while we are short of food?" quoth the Pathan and seized the bird.

The next day the farmer brought another rooster to sell. "What do you feed that bird that he is so big?" demanded a Baluch soldier of the Pakistan army "Sir, I feed it with ghee," replied the farmer.

"How dare you waste ghee on a bird while we are short of food!" swore the Baluchi as he seized the bird.

The next day the poor farmer brought his last remaining rooster to the market. This time a Punjabi Mussalman soldier asked him, "What do you feed that bird that it is so big?" The Bangla farmer joined the palms of his hands and pleaded, "Sir, I don't give him any feed. I just give him two paise every day to buy whatever he likes in the market."

So far the wittiest barb fired at me came after our issue on abortion. Wrote a wisecrack: "If your mother had the good sense we would have been spared an editor like you." *Touche*.

I had never met Piloo Mody before I became a Member of Parliament. He was a weighty man with a mind as nimble as his body. During one of the interludes in an otherwise very serious conference, he regaled us with his plea for a Parsi State. This is how it went:

"This country should be handed over to the Parsis —on a Managing Agency basis. We will charge only a 5% Managing Agency Commission, which is a hell of a lot less than the Government of India spends on administration."

"For this, we will give you a clean, honest, impartial and non-discriminatory government. There are only a hundred thousand of us, and we will satiate ourselves with corruption and nepotism. There will still be enough left over for everyone else."

"We are the most non-communal community in the world. We believe that either you are a Parsi or you are not. If you are not, it makes no hoot of a différence who you are."

"Go ahead ... go breaking up this country into a hundred parts. Finally our turn will come."

"Then we will demand a Parsi State, consisting of the area from Kemp's Corner to Teen Batti (about two square miles).

"But, as we cannot have a sovereign independent country of Banganga on the other side, you will have to throw in Banganga with the Parsi State. We need servants!"

The latest joke from Czechoslovakia is a dialogue between an official assigned to gauge public opinion and a peasant. The official made his questionnaire as simple as possible for the rustic's mind: "Now, Jan, if you were asked to make three wishes for your country, what would they be?"

"First, I would wish the People's Liberation Army of the People's Republic of Red China to occupy Czechoslovakia."

The official refused to be put out of countenance. "And what would be your second wish?"

"My second wish would be that the People's Liberation Army of the People's Republic of Red China should occupy Czechoslovakia."

"Okay, okay! That's the same wish twice. What would be your third wish?"

"My third wish would be that the People's Liberation Army of the People's Republic of Red China should occupy Czechoslovakia for the third time."

"Now, aren't you being a little perverse? Why would you wish your country to be invaded and occupied three times by a foreign army?"

"That is very simple," replied Jan, "the people's Liberation Army of Red China would first have to march across and occupy the Soviet Union three times before it could get to us. That would teach the Russians what it means to be under foreign occupation."

It is true our Cabinet Ministers have shed some of their self-esteem and delusions of grandeur. It is said that one of them did in fact go to his Guru to make a confession that he had incurred the sin of vanity.

"What makes you think that?" asked the Guru.

"Because every morning, when I look into the mirror as I am shaving, I think what a wonderful and important person I am."

"Never fear, my dear Minister," came the reassuring reply, "that is not a sin. It's only a mistake."

Nurul Alam from Silchar sends me a few lovely samples of bureaucratic wit of the days of British Raj. One is an entry made by an executive engineer in the visitors' book of a Circuit House:

"The verandah of the Circuit House badly needs railings. During my momentary absence, a cow ate up some estimates which I had left lying on a table in the verandah." Below this note was the Commissioner's observation: "I find it hard to believe that even cows could swallow PWD estimates."

In another Circuit House book another executive engineer had noted: "The washbasin should be immediately replaced. I could not wash my face properly for want of proper facilities." Against this entry is a marginal note in the commissioner's beautiful hand: "SDO will replace the washbasin at once. The executive engineer had to wash his face in tears during his last visit to this station."

The prize remark is against a complaint that the latrine was too far away from the bungalow. "He should have started earlier," wrote the wit.

All these are attributed to one Mr. Bentink.

I have so many amusing anecdotes on Prem Kirpal, his love of good food and wine (he drank more liquor off me than off himself), his vast collection of unread books, his absent mindedness etc. However I'll break the vow and tell you of one about his habit of talking loudly over the phone. We were sitting on the crowded lobby of a hotel in Madrid when he was summoned to the telephone booth in a corner of the hall. Without shutting the door Kirpal began to yell into the phone: "Lizbeth! Hello! How are you?" People in the lobby stopped talking. Everyone was amused. He came back and announced to me, "That was Elizabeth Adiseshiah, you know?"

"Yes," I replied sarcastically, "so does everyone else in the lobby."

"Was I talking very loudly? Her hotel is five miles away, you know!"

It reminded me of Winston Churchill's retort to a Minister who shared the next cubicle and was wont to talk at the top of his voice. He sent his secretary to tell the Minister to lower his voice. The secretary came back and explained, "Sir, Mr Brown is talking to Scotland."

"I know," replied Winston Churchill, "tell him to use the telephone."

The following news item is taken from an English provincial paper:

"When a disaster occurs, the Red Cross Society is always glad to help— especially money. But some gifts can cause embarassment. When 200 cases of bras were sent as a well-meaning gift to Pakistan, the problem which they caused was solved by cutting them in half to make two rice bowls."

96

In Bombay I once changed my telephone number. For some inexplicable reason, my new number was the old number of an elderly Parsi couple. So six of the seven calls I take go somewhat as follow:

"Hormazd?"

"No."

"Bearer , *Seth kah gayach?*"

Bearer indeed! I break into my how-haw Oxbridge. "I am afraid this is not Mr. Hormazd's number any more. I do not know how he is, nor his telephone number. Please ring 'Enquiries!'"

A week later, apparently, word must have gone round that Hormazd was ill. No sooner would I plug in the instrument than calls would start pouring in. I avoided plugging till after midnight, when I was sure Hormazd and his friends were fast asleep.

The telephone rang. I switched on the bed lamp. It was 3 a.m. My temper was high. My thinking capacity was very low. The Devil got inside me. A lady's voice demanded to know the health of Mr Hormazd.

In my best Parsi Gujarati, I replied: *"Arre, soon kehoon mai. Evan to rate gujri gaya"* - He died last night.

"O khadai! Soon Kaoch Bawa!" came the wail *"Soon thayyun?* What happened."

"Kon Jane - kai poochhoj na - please...."

I put down the receiver.

I realised too late I had brought trouble on my head. Thereafter the telephone rang again and again. The frantic queries were all the same.

"Hormazd ne soon thai gayyun ..... We are coming over right away ... *Mrs Hormazdji ne bolawoni please-* Call Mrs Homi."

I grew tired of replying. *"Hormazd ne Dungarwadi lai gaya chhe.* Mrs Homi is heart-broken. She cannot speak."

But the calls continued. Whenever I plugged the phone in—it rang.

On the third day, I decided to put an end to the nuisance by yelling into the receiver: "Hormazd, whoever the ass is, is not dead and I couldn't care less whether he dies or lives. But, for God's sake, leave me alone!"

I plugged the phone in and waited. It rang. I picked up the receiver, but before I could begin, an irate old lady's voice came through with searing abuse:

"*Marere mua - Luchcha, Laffanga,* you've been spreading the news that my poor Homi is dead. *Mare taro baap, taro baap no baap tara badha* dear ones! I shall report you to the police. I shall have you arrested...."

George Brown, when he was England's Foreign Minister, was being entertained in Paris by his Ambassador, Sir Patrick Reilly. The chief guests were the Prime Minister of France and his wife. During the course of this very formal dinner, Mr Brown turned to the French Prime Minister's wife and complimented her on her looks by describing her as "most beddable". The hostess was scandalised. "Really, Mr Brown!" she reprimanded her husband's boss "hardly the thing to say to the wife of Prime Minister!" Brown ignored her and continued to address the chief guest's wife. "Surely, Madam, other people have paid you similar compliments!" The French lady retorted in the typically charming French way, *"Ouis Monsieur,* but never before coffee."

"Mr and Mrs Bunny Reuben request the pleasure of your company to the wedding of their daughter Neena Deborah with Dr. Robert". I promptly wrote on the card "accept/enter in diary". I arrived at 6.30 p.m. at the grounds of the Gymkhana Club. All very garishly lit up with a profusion of coloured lights and noisy with music blaring out of microphones. I couldn't see my hosts nor the nuptial pair; nor any film stars or journalists I expected to see at a film journalists' party. But it was a mixed bag. Some Semitic types (Bunny is a Bene Israel Jew), some Maratha ladies with saris tucked into their massive posteriors (Mrs Reuben is Maharashtrian). And a sprinkling of Sethias, Sardars, Sindhis, Mianbhais, Makapaos and Bawajis.

I sat alone sipping my fizzy aerated water hoping to spot my hosts. Then my patience ran out and I decided to bless the marital pair now posted at the gate and take my leave. As is my wont, I planted a kiss on the bride's cheek, called the groom a lucky bugger and went home. Next morning I discovered I had been to the wrong wedding reception, ate somebody else's ice-cream and kissed a stranger's daughter. Such is life in a city where a dozen wedding receptions take place every evening.

This I picked up in the Central Hall of Parliament. Apparently President Zail Singh was operated on the same Texan hospital as his predecessor Sanjiva Reddy. When taken to the operating theatre, the chief surgeon asked our Rashtrapati : "Are you ready?"

"No I am not Reddy", replied Gyaniji, "I am Zail Singh."

"You know why India lost the hockey final to Pakistan." he asked.

"No. You tell me."

"It was a part of the Simla Agreement between Mrs Gandhi and President Bhutto."

I recall an incident during one of the General Elections when an unusually self-righteous and aggressive Janata candidate confronted a staunch Congressite. "After all the evil deeds done by the Congress party during the Emergency how can you vote for that party?" he asked. Unabashed the Congressman replied: "I am a Congressman because my father and before him his father were for the Congress".

"Aha!" exclaimed the Janata candidate triumphantly, hoping to squash the voter. "If your father was a donkey and before him his father also a donkey, what would that make you?"

"That, Sir" retorted the voter, "would make me Janata."

Duleepsinhji was playing in a test match for England against Australia. An English spectator turned to an Australian sitting next to him and asked: "Have you any Princes in your team?" The Aussie admitted they had none. "We have had many," boasted the Englishman. "Now take this fellow Duleep! As blue-blooded as any aristocrat in the world. And a damn fine cricketer too!" Just then Duleep hit a sixer. "See what I mean?" exploded the Englishman. The next ball knocked Duleep's centre wicket. The Englishman yelled: "He's out! The bloody nigger!"

A reader, Srinivasan Sampath, sends me the following: Yeardly Norton, an Irishman, was a leading criminal lawyer of Madras known for his biting sarcasm. He was appearing on behalf on a plaintiff in a very sensational case involving two important personalities in a case of adultery. To drive home his point, without wasting time of the court, he said: "Your Honour, the case is very simple. But in a case of adultery, you will agree that it is difficult to prove factual reality in pictures unless a three dimensional camera is fixed to every bed room since a mere peep through the key-hole will never suffice. But, in all fairness, if a man and woman are always found closeted in a room for hours at a stretch, neither Your Lordship nor I would expect them to be reading the Bible or Geeta". Norton won his case.

A friend returned from Eastern (Communist) Europe narrated the following story during the rounds in these countries. One morning a school girl came to her teacher and said very proudly: "Our cat has had a litter of six kittens and they are all Communists." The teacher was impressed with the child and invited the Inspector to visit the school and see for himself how well-doctrinated her students were. A week later the inspector arrived. "Tell the gentleman about your cat," the teacher asked her student.

"She has had six kittens and they are all democrats", said the girl.

"What!" exclaimed the teacher aghast and let down, "last week you told me they were all Communists. What makes you say now they are democrats?"

"Since then their eyes have opened," replied the student.

Here two similar linguistic lapses committed by men expected to have better acquaintance with English. One was the late Radha Raman, once a mighty pillar of the Delhi Administration. At a buffet dinner where the Prime Minister was pressed him to help himself to some food. "Not yet," replied Raman, I'll eat only after the Prime Minister has passed away."

Once I was hosting a lunch for a minister. When I offered the dessert to him, he wagged his head and said: "No, thank you! I am quite fed up."

Vansant Sathe intending to compliment Sharada Prasad, author of the text, and Satyan for the photographs in the lavishly produced book on Karnataka remarked: "You two have immoralised Karnataka!" Vansant certainly immortalised himself.

My favourite story of a linguistic *faux pas* is of a friend who broke wind somewhat loudly in mixed company. Overcome with embarrassment he stuttered: "Sorry, it was a slip of the tongue."

Mr Rifaquat Ali sends me an anecdote based on the Bengali way of pronunciation of words. A Sardarji, newly arrived in Calcutta, was invited by his Bengali neighbour to what he thought was to be a *bhojan*. He ate nothing all day, so he could do justice to rice and *macherjhol* (fish curry) and *rosogollas*. He arrived at the appointed time and was regaled with a feast of hymn singing—*bhajan!*

Once upon a time there lived a very powerful Nawab Sahib who loved vegetable gardens and courtiers. One day he had his throne placed in midst of a patch of brinjals. "Allah be praised!" he exclaimed. "What a beautiful vegetable is this brinjal! What exquisite shape! What smoothness of texture! What colouring!"

"Ala Hazrat!" chorused the courtiers. "Indeed Allah has made the brinjal the most beautiful of all vegetables in the world".

"But it does not taste very good," remarked the Nawab Sahib. "And doctors say it has little food value."

"Exactly so!" agreed the courtiers. "It is the foulest of foods. It is better to take poison than eat a brinjal."

"You are a strange lot," said the Nawab Sahib irately. "When I praise the brinjal, you heap superlatives on it. When I say a word in criticism, you execrate it in equally strong language. What kind of people are you?"

The courtiers replied in courtly courtesy: "Ala Hazrat, we eat your salt, not that of the brinjal."

A wealthy Maheshwari, the richest of the Marwari community, was complaining about his wife's spendthrift habits to a friend. "One day she asked me for ten rupees, the next day she asked me for twenty and this morning she wanted twenty-five. She is the limit."

"She certainly is," agreed the friend. "What did she do with all that money?"

"Main kya jaanoon" (how should I know), replied the wealthy man. "I never gave her any."

Once upon a time there was a nonconforming swallow who decided not to fly south for the winter. However, when the weather turned very cold, he reluctantly started to fly southwards. In a short time ice began to form on its wings and it fell to earth in a barnyard frozen still. A cow passed by and crapped on the little swallow. The swallow thought it was the end. But the dung warmed it and defrosted its wings. Warm and happy, able to breathe, it started to chirp. Just then a large Tom cat came by and hearing the chirping, found out where it was coming from, clawed away the dung and swallowed the swallow.

Moral: Everyone who shits on you is not necessarily your enemy: everyone who gets you out of the shit is not necessarily your friend, and if you're warm and happy in a pile of shit, keep your mouth shut.

Contributed by Shridhar Vyas Bangalore

An inspector of schools went to a government-aided school and put the following question to students of sixth class: "You have read the *Ramayana*. Tell me who broke the Shiva's *dhanush?* Only one boy raised his hand: "Sir, I do not know who broke it but it was not me."

The inspector turned to the teacher and reprimanded him for not having done his job. The teacher replied: "Sir, the boy is very naughty. I am sure it was he who broke it, but will not admit it."

The inspector went to the headmaster and narrated the whole story. After hearing him the headmaster said: "Why make a fuss about such a petty thing. Whatever is broken is broken for ever. While paying us the grant you may deduct the price of a *new dhanush* and pay the balance."

Contributed by R. R. Bajaj

Friends have sent me some more examples of linguistic lapses made by men expected to know better. Apparently Bombay University has a Professor Spooner of its own. I am forbidden from mentioning his name but permitted to quote him. Once when this esteemed professor had stayed with a family and wanted to thank his hostess for her hospitality he said: "Thank you very much for all your hostility".

The same professor giving a farewell talk to a batch of students going abroad advised them:"Do in Rome as Romeos do".

From Bombay again comes this malapropism. A gentleman wiping the perspiration of his brow remarked:; "In Bombay it is prostitution and more prostitution."

Commander A.K.B. Menon has sent me some examples of mispronunciations of English words by Tamilians, Gujaratis, Bengalis, and Punjabis. Of these the Punjabis come of worst with *laiyyer for* leisure, *playyer* for pleasure and *maiyyur* for good measure. I had heard all these mispronunciations but not their role in the reverse. There was this Punjabi minister (they do not always have to be Sardarjis) who on the eve of his goodwill mission to Birmingham, was advised by his Tamilian secretary: "Şarr, be careful with your pronunciation of English words. Don't say *diviyun,* it is division, not *Tallyviyyun, it is television, not maiyyur* it is measure". And so on. The minister made careful note of these tricky words. On arrival at Birmingham airport he was welcomed by the Lord Mayor of the city. The Punjabi minister, extending his hand, said, "How nice to meet you, Lord Measure!"

Share a joke with Khushwant Singh

If you have a joke, a humorous anecdote or a funny incident, which is original and you would like to share it with Khushwant Singh and his million admirers, send it to us today. If selected, it would be printed in the next edition of Khushwant Singh's Joke Book.

... and a million others

Remember

- Each joke or anecdote must be neatly typed or written on a separate sheet of paper in about 125-150 words.
- Do not type or write on both sides of the sheet. Write on one side only.
- Send your jokes to :

  Khushwant Singh's Joke Book
  c/o **Orient Paperbacks**
  Madarsa Road, Kashmere Gate
  DELHI - 110 006

- Each contribution received would be acknowledged.
- Each selected contribution would be acknowledged and included in the next edition of **Khushwant Singh's Joke Book** along with the name of the contributor.

I offered a prize of Rs. five for the best family planning slogan. Quite a few readers responded. Most ignored my request that their slogans should be witty not vulgar. Obviously I cannot publish those that transgressed limits of decency. Two sent by R.K. Puri from Calcutta were on the borderline: "Copulate merrily but not populate verily." And its variation: "India's crying need—copulation without population."

K.P. Lahiri of Gauhati sent in five entries of which one I disqualify for near-vulgarity: "Whatever F may stand for, consider P for preventing child-birth." The one which just misses the mark is meant to be pinned on the wall above the pillow: "Child producing is injurious to health and happiness." Then there is a woman's lib slogan pertinent to child-bearing: "Ban nine month confinement."

I am not sure how much appeal the following will have for a newly married couple: "A baby is sweet, a baby is great joy. If you want one, why not a baby toy?" I liked Lahiri's: "Make an issue a non-issue" but feel that it is somewhat obscure.

L.R. Ferrao of Goa suggests adopting "Matrimony—matter of money: additional two—blissful atrimony." I do not understand the play on words nor the message. A.H. Rashid of Pune has sent in three slogans, all passably good:" If love makes the world go round, then too many children make it flat." "Let love flow out of you—not babies" (surely a variation of make love not babies! and 'love-making is easy baby making is costly').

Rattan Kumar Dutt of Calcutta has sent in two entries: "Promise her anything but make your next IOU and IUD" and "Loop before you leap." I have an uneasy feeling that I have seen his second entry somewhere. However, I will send my five ruppes to Rattan Kumar Dutt in the hope that if some reader proves that "Loop before you leap" is not original, he will return my money to me, so that I can pass it on to the author of a gem in Punjabi-English I saw printed on the back of a cycle-rickshaw:

"Aurat hovey teep taap
Do dey badd full istaap."

(A wench should be tip top, After two, a full stop).

Once at a *mushaira* while other poets were reciting their compositions, the cord of Firaq's pajama snapped. When his turn came, he proceeded to recite while sitting down. The crowd clamoured: "Please get up and come to the mike". Firaq stayed glued to his *takia* and replied *"Khawateen-o-Hazrat* (ladies and gentlemen) the cord of my pajama has snapped. If you want to hear my ghazals you will have to let me remain seated. If, however, you wish to have *deedar* (darshan) of something else, I will be glad to stand up." They brought the mike to where he was seated.

Firaq was pestered by aspiring poets to write prefaces to their works. One such poet who was over-sure of himself approached Firaq and by way of self-introduction said: "Firaq Sahib, my poems have been published in all the leading Urdu magazines and journals in the country. No doubt you must have read many of them."

Firaq replied: "All these magazines and journals you speak of also carry advertisements of medicines to cure piles; do you expect me to have read all these?" (Incidentally, Firaq suffered from piles and some of his jokes are about the pain they caused him in his fundament.)

Ravi Kathpalia, First Secretary in our High Commission in London, narrated the following experience: His wife and he were invited to a small intimate dinner party by a lady who had once combined glamour with skill to dominate the women's tennis scene of the world. The conversation drifted from the field of tennis but suddenly the tennis champion asked:

"What religion do you belong to?"

"Try and guess," he said.

"You are not Christians, surely?"

"No."

"You are not Jews, I know. You must be Buddhists, aren't you?"

"No, but you are getting nearer."

I've got it. You are Muslims."

"No, you haven't," he said "But you should get it next time."

"Oh, but of course, you are Hindus."

"You've got it. Well done."

And then she turned round to her little girl and proclaimed: "I told you, darling. They are Hindus who believe in Islam!"

American: Have you heard, Americans have gone to the moon?

Pakistani: Allah be praised for small mercies!

But not all of them have gone.

Pakistani: What are so many Russians doing in Kabul for the last five years?

American: They are looking for the man who invited them.

The Sikhs have always known it as *karhah pershad* the divine offering. It is a batter made of equal parts of flour (or *soojee*), sugar and ghee. It is *halwa* elevated to the status of a *prasad* (offering to the gods), because it is served at the end of every religious service. If you are a good Sikh and have not broken any of the vows taken at baptism and are lucky enough to be amongst the first five to be served you are entitled to two helpings. I barely qualify for a quarter of what is given to the faithful.

It used to be my favourite sweet dish. A well-cooked *halwa* of *soojee* with raisins and almonds can match the best of desserts. During the rainy season, particularly the chill of the winter monsoon, the very thought of a steaming mound of *halwa* can make one's mouth water. I recall one winter when I was caught in a shower and chilled to the bone a Tamilian classmate at college took me home to change into a dry shirt. His mother gave me a platter full of what I thought was *halwa*. No sooner than I put a large spoonful in my mouth, I spat it out. I was expecting it to be sweet, it turned out to be salted. I pretended that in my eagerness to savour it I had burnt my mouth. That was my first introduction *uppuma*. Since then I have cultivated a taste for it and prefer it to the sweetened stuff.

Halwa has produced an amusing Khalistani joke. Two ardent supporters were discussing the wonderful time they would have after Khalistan is established: "We will eat *karhah pershad* every day," said one.

"But the doctor has forbidden me from eating *karhah pershad*," protested the other, "I am diabetic."

"Once we have our Khalistan, whether you have diabetes—shiabetis and whether or not you like it, you will have to eat *karhah pershad* every day."

"**I** am the most unfortunate man in the world; my *kismet* is ruined," cried Lala Dhani Ram as he slapped his forehead.

"Lalaji, what's happened?" asked his friends.

"What's happened? My daughter's gone and married that good-for-nothing fellow who does not know how to drink or gamble."

"You call that bad *kismet?*" they asked somewhat bewildered. "You should consider yourself lucky to have a son-in-law who does not drink or gamble."

"Who said he does not drink or gamble? He does both. I said he does not know how to do them."

I once coined an aphorism which I thought was quite clever because it was impossible: "They were twins, but one of them was a bastard." Now I discover that this is in fact possible and a woman can bear twins sired by different fathers. This can happen when a woman has sexual intercourse with two men within a short interval. Her ovary fertilised by the first man can be re-fertilised by the second man and thus yield twins. This rare phenomenon is known as "the milkman effect." In case you don't understand why they have picked on the poor milk supplier let me tell you. In most of the western world milkmen deliver bottles in the morning after husbands have left for work and wives are still in their flimsy negligees. Many a wife has been tempted to offer her milkman a warm cup of tea in the kitchen followed by a session in a warmer bed. Our gynaecologists might discover similar offsprings of the *gowalla* effect on Indian housewives who prefer buying milk from Gujars rather than get bottled milk from the dairy booth.

This exchange took place many years ago between the then Finance Minister John Mathai, and Acharya Kripalani. The Acharya is renowned for his acid tongue. He was going for the civil service and injected a particularly waspish anecdote about a young man who having knocked at many doors to find a job returned crestfallen to his father. The father reassured him: "I know you are a no good son of a gun. No one in his senses will employ you. But don't lose hope, you can always get a government job; they are meant for worthless people like you."

John Mathai was quick to reply: "Having heard the Acharya's observation with great respect, I am coming to the conclusion that Acharyaji is fast becoming ripe for a government job."

A Haryana Jat, who had been irritated by his failure to answer any of the riddles put to him by a clever *bania*, said angrily: "All right now you answer this riddle: What is that is hung on a wall, is red, drips and speaks?"

After a while the *bania* admitted he did not know the answer.

"It is a picture!", said the Jat triumphantly.

"A picture? It can be hung on a wall but it is not always red," protested the *bania*.

"Then paint it red".

"A picture doesn't drip; its dry," protested the *bania* again.

"Put fresh paint on it and it will drip".

"But whoever heard of a picture talk!"

"That's right!", replied the Jat, "I added that to make sure a cunning *bania* like you would not get the answer".

There's the story of a newly rich Punjabi couple who having come into money were forever boasting of their acquisitions: a brand new imported car (not a second hand one sold by S.T.C.), video-casettes, hi-fi-, original paintings. "And, of course, our food is always cooked in *asli ghee*", said the wife proudly,"*no dalda shalda* in our kitchen".

Once holidaying at Juhu Beach in Bombay the husband went out of his depth and was just saved from drowning. A doctor was quickly summoned. "Nothing to worry", exclaimed the medico, "I will give him artificial respiration and he will be all right in a jiffy".

"No you won't", said the wife, "for my husband it will have to be real respiration or nothing".

Some sane words of advice for a nation of gossip mongers that we have become today. They are from no less a person than the sage Socrates.

One day a friend who came to visit the philosopher asked him: "Socrates, have you heard the rumour that is going round the city like wildfire?"

"Before you tell me what it is," interjected Socrates, "have you checked whether or not it is correct?"

"No," admitted the visitor, "but I have heard it talked about in every street and at every crossroad."

"In that case, tell me is it good news?"

"No, it is not".

"Will spreading bad news do good to anyone?"

"No, it will not."

"In that case," said Socrates. "do not bother to tell me what it is. Why do you lend your ears to news that are neither true nor good? Friend, life has so much good to offer, why not ponder over it?"

"You must have a lot of number two." Being slow on the uptake, I didn't catch what the cab-driver Sardarji meant. "What is number two?" I asked.

"Black."

I took umbrage. "What makes you think I have lots of number two?" I demanded.

"You are staying in a hotel which charges Rs 500 a night for a single room. In this joint a sister-loving bottle of beer costs Rs 15. Only those who have number two stay in such places."

I protested and named a well-known and respected politician who was staying in the same hotel. The Sardarji was not impressed. *"he is a dus numberiya!—* You know what a number ten is?"

"A *badmash.* I have neither number two nor am I a number *dus"*, I protested again. "And there are many others staying in this very hotel who are neither one or the other."

"Name them," he challenged. "Anyone who goes to a five-star hotel is either two or *dus.* Or he is in the *gaurmint* or with a *kompanee* that makes a lot of black. It is the same thing."

I decided to speak sharply. "Sardarji, it is all very well for you to talk in this way about other people. What about you and your taxi driving fraternity? How often do you fiddle with your meters? The board in the hotel says: Santa-Cruz to Church Gate Rs 36. Your meter reads Rs 45."

He was unabashed. "When all the world does 420, why should we poor taxi drivers be the only ones who don't do 420?"

I didn't know how to answer that one. I decided to throw the ball in his court: "Why do you talk in numbers? Number two, number ten, number 420?"

"Because I am *Sava Lakh"* (equal to 1,25,000) he replied, stroking his long beard.

Question: Why have all the dance Academies in Pakistan been closed down?

Answer: Because from now on *sarkar hee sab ko nachaaegee* (the government will make everyone dance).

A Punjabi peasant was travelling by train with his two infant sons. When the conductor asked him for their tickets, he produced a half ticket. "You are three; you must have three tickets: one full and two halves," said the conductor angrily.

"When we three travel together, I always buy a half ticket," replied the peasant naively.

The conductor lost his temper, "You dunderhead, how can three persons become half? Just explain that to me."

"Simple," replied the peasant clambering on the upper berth. "See one over two equals half."

Contributed by Harjeet Kaur, New Delhi.

Apparently Hindi translations of English titles continue to be fabricated for the sheer fun they provide. We were familiarised with the All India Lawn Tennis Tournament as *Akhil Bharatiya Ghaas Phoos Gaindballa Muthbhed*. An equally amusing rendering in Hindi of a game of ping pong is *Batti kay neechay, takht kay oopar, idhar say thakaa-thak, udhar say thakaa-thak*.

115

This story, which appeared in *The Times* (London) highlights the humiliations the civil servants have to suffer at the hands of ministers. There was this civil servant who retired after 40 years of slogging in his office. He rented a small cottage near a village and went into a self-imposed *Vanprastha*. The villagers became very curious about him. But all they saw was that every morning a boy came to his door, rang the bell and spoke a sentence. The civil servant replied with a sentence and handed him a coin. When curiosity got the better of the village folk, they approached the boy and asked him what passed between them: "Nothing much" replied the lad, "he's hired me to ring his bell and say to him "Sir, the Minister wants to see you!" And he replies: "Tell the bloody Minister to bugger off. For this he pays me ten pence a time."

It is a long time since I heard a joke about a stupid minister of government. For some obscure reasons some minister who are by no means stupid had a lot of jokes fastened on them whereas others who are obvious screwballs went scot-free. Two names readily come to mind. There was Sardar Dasaundha Singh, who became a minister in Sir Sikandar Hayat's Unionist government in the Punjab. He had been a prominent lawyer at Ludhiana before he became a minister. He was also a very modest man. I recall a remark he made when I went to congratulate him on his success. "This is a strange world." he said "even a man who accidentally treads on a partridge gets to be known as a great *Shikari.*" By all accounts Dasaundha Singh acquitted himself well as a minister. Nevertheless all manner of jokes were tagged on to him.

We had a sitting duck in Raj Narain. Although much fun was poked at him it was more about his clowning than his failure to grasp simple problems. This one has been sent to me of his days as the Minister of Health. He was questioned about a report claiming that the incidence of deaths from cholera had come down from 9 to 5.7 per thousand. "Sir, we can understand nine deaths and we can understand five deaths, but what exactly do 5.7 deaths mean?" asked a newspaperman.

Raj Narain replied: "That means that five are dead and seven on the point of death."

A lawyer was appearing for the prosecution in a murder case where the accused's wife, a prostitute, was giving evidence of alibi to the effect that her husband was with her in her house at the time of the murder. Their home was some distance from the brothel where the lady carried on her business and where the murder had taken place at night—the usual working hour in her profession. He proceeded to cross-examine her: "How is it that you were not at your place of business that night?"

"I practise my profession during the day-time," she replied somewhat tartly. "How can that be? Don't your patrons seek you at hours usual in the profession?"

"Oh, no, Sir," she replied coquettishly. "Only goondas, badmashes and other lowly types visit brothels at night. Respectable gentlemen like yourself come in day-time."

It is the favourite topic in the Central Hall of Parliament where reputations of the high and mighty are sold for the price of a subsidised *masala dosa*. The recent corruption debate was summarised by a journalist friend in the following words: "What you give to the minister is a *nazrana* (offering); to an official a *shukrana* (thanks giving); to the clerk a *mehantana* (work compensation) and to the chaprasi, *baksheesh* (tip)."

"But *baksheesh* does not rhyme with *nazrana shukrana* and *mehantana,*" I protested.

He paused for a while, plucked a hair out of his sparse beard and replied: "In that case call the chaprasi's share a *shurooana* (beginning) or card *pahunchana* because he is the first to introduce you to the clerk, official and the minister."

A Nihang decided to stop an express train at a non-stop station. He stood in the middle of the railtrack brandishing his *kirpan* and spear and yelling defiance at the oncoming train. A crowd watched the confrontation with bated breath. When the engine driver noticed the Nihang on the track and realised he would not be able to stop the train in time, he blew his whistle as frantically as he could. Just as the engine was almost upon him, the Nihang jumped aside and let the train pass.

"What happened Nihangji?" asked the onlookers. "Did you take fright?"

"Never!" replied the Nihang with bravado. "You see how I made it scream (*cheekaan kaddh dittiyan!*). A Nihang never kills anyone who cries for mercy."

"You become what you eat", she pronounced with an air of finality. "You eat bad things, you become a bad man; you drink liquor, you become a drunkard".

I was taken aback by this verbal assault designed to persuade me to give up drinking. This Morarji Desai was a pretty miss who though somewhat confused in her thinking was also very lovable. I took the offensive: "So Muslims and Christians who eat beef become cows and buffaloes; Hindus who eat mutton become goats; Sikhs who eat pork, become pigs. And the rest of the world who eat all these things become some kind of stew made of beef, mutton and pork!"

She stood her ground. "Any kind of meat is bad; any kind of liquor is bad."

It was like breaking one's head against the wall of obscurantism. The notion of food being *Satvik, Rajsik* or *Tamsik* is deeply rooted in the Indian mind. Meat and liquor are *tamsik:* ergo, they must be avoided. It is no use arguing that *lassan* (garlic) and *heeng* (asafoetida) are also *tamsik* and yet recommended by doctors including vaids and hakeems for digestive problems. I turned the tables on her by asking her what she could recommend as the most wholesome diet. "Fresh vegetables are the best," she replied.

"So you eat cabbage and become like a cabbage", I remarked.

Driving back from Kasauli to Delhi I once took a new route which was more picturesque as it ran along the foothills. However, at many intersections there were no roadsigns to indicate the right direction. At one major crossing not knowing which one to take, I espied a peasant sitting in the shade.

"*Bhai sahib*, can you tell me where this road goes to? I asked.

"*Kya maloom?* (How should I know?)."

What about this one on the left, where does it lead to?" I asked

"*Kya maloom.*"

For the one on the right?

"*Kya maloom.*"

I lost my patience and shouted; "*Kucch to maloom hoga* (you must know something). Which way are you going?"

He replied with composure: "I am not going anywhere. I just came here to see motor cars go by."

One morning an elderly matron boarded a bus and occupied a seat without buying a ticket. An irate conductor addressed her rudely, "*Budhiya* — old woman—first buy your ticket before you sit down." The lady rasped back: "First learn to speak politely and then ask for money for a ticket. Instead of calling me a *budhiya* you should have said: '*Jiji* (elder sister), please buy a ticket'." The humbled conductor had to repeat the lady's words before he got the fare. Everyone was amused. At the next stop, a hefty *sadhu* boarded the bus. This time the conductor got his own back. He addressed the sadhu very loudly: "*Jeejaji* (brother-in-law) you can take the vacant seat next to *Jiji.*"

A Pakistani VIP staying in a five-star establishment in Delhi was accosted by pimps and ladies of pleasure in the corridors of his hotel (the sort that often exercise the minds of members of Parliament). He also toured the city and saw the sorry state of our roads. "Delhi reminds me very much of the early days in Karachi in 1947", he remarked. "How's that?" asked his Indian host. "It's all ditches and bitches," he replied.

What he said sounded much better in Hindustani than it does in English.

Sindhis are known both for their sharp practices as well as for their clanishness: they drive hard bargains but also help fellow-Sindhis to find employment. The following story was told to me by a Sindhi businessman on a visit to Hong Kong. He wanted to have a silk suit made and went to a Sindhi tailor's shop at the airport which advertised suits made to measure in a couple of hours. The visiting businessman selected the material and asked how much it cost. The tailor replied: "Sir, seeing you are a fellow Sindhi I will offer you a special price. A suit of this material costs 200 Hong Kong dollars as you can see clearly marked on the label. I charge everyone else two hundred dollars but not a fellow Sindhi. I won't ask for 190 dollars not even 180 dollars. For you it will be 170 dollars not a cent more."

"Why should you lose money on me just because I happen to be a fellow-Sindhi," replied the visitor. "So what should I offer for this suit? 70 dollars? That I would to a non-Sindhi tailor. 80 dollars? That would be insulting a Sindhi brother. I offer you 90 dollars and not a cent less."

"Okay. That's a deal," replied the tailor.

A well-known politician had the misfortune of locking himself out of his car leaving the keys inside. After trying out other keys and prodding the tightly shut window panes, he thought he would insert a wire in the key hole and twist it round: if car thieves could open them that way why not he? Unfortunately, while he was at it, a policeman came up and grabbed him by the arm: "Whose car are you trying to steal?" he demanded gruffly.

"It's my car', replied the politician somewhat taken aback. The policeman slapped him across the face as well as cast reflections on the fellow's relations with his mother and sister. Screaming with rage the outraged politician returned the compliments to the constable and showed him the label on the windscreen which proclaimed his name and eminence in public life. It was the turn of the policeman to apologise and make amends: "Sahib you must forgive me! You must be the only politician who does not know how to break open a lock."

In a crowded railway compartment one berth was occupied by a man covered from head to foot with his bedsheet. A porter entered and without much ado proceeded to belabour the recumbent figure with blows and abuse: "O! *Jagtara, teri maan di.; O! Jagtara, teri bhain di....* etc. etc. After a while the other passengers intervened, uncovered the recumbent man's face and asked him why he was taking all the fisticuffs and abuse without a protest.

"The joke is on this fellow" he replied, "he'll soon tire of beating me and in any case I am not Jagtara."

Sri A.K. Rajvanshi of Meerut has drawn my attention to an odd phenomenon in the English way of spelling proper names related to Hinduism. He castigates the practice of adding the letter A to the end of Hindu names as "rape of Hinduism". I don't understand why he should feel so strongly about it but I am greatly intrigued and request readers to suggest explanations. Why for instance is Ram spelt as Rama, Krishn as Krishna but Mohammed or Nanak never as Mohammeda or Nanaka? Why is Ramayan spelt as Ramayana, Mahabharat as Mahabharata but Quran never spelt as Qurana or Granth as Grantha? Why is Ashok spelt as Ashoka, Harsh as Harsha but never Babar nor Akbar as Babara or Akbara?

Rajvanshi may well amend Shakespeare's denunciation of the last letter of the English alphabet: "Thou whoreson zed, thou unnecessary letter?" *(King Lear)* replacing Z by A. A may not be the illegitimate child of a lady of easy virtue but it certainly is an unnecessary appendage to Hindu names.

An essay on *Geese* submitted by a school-boy reads:

Geese is a low heavy set bird which is mostly meat and feathers. His head is one side and he sits on the other. Geese can't sing much on account of the dampness of the moisture. He's got no between the toes and he's got a little balloon in his stomach to keep him from sinking.

Some geese, when they get big, has curls on their tails and is called ganders. Ganders don't have to sit and hatch but just sit and loaf and go swimming. If I was goose, I would rather be a gander.

Courtesy by R.K. Murthi.

Shortly before taking over as Air Chief from Arjan Singh, P.C. Lal had to spend long hours being briefed about his new charge. As a result he had to stay late in office to clear his own files. The poor Air Force jawan on guard duty at Air Headquarters had to stay at his post till after 10.30 p.m. After a week of suffering he made bold to address the new Air Chief-to-be: "Sir, may I be allowed to ask you a question?" Being permitted to do so he continued: "You stay in office till very late, whereas Air Marshal Arjan Singh left punctually at 5 p.m. Is it that you have not yet understood your work? Or has the work-load increased?"

Thereafter P.C. Lal left his office on time.

A young Punjabi couple who I hardly knew insisted that I come to their house-warming party. I went suitably armed with compliments for the hostess and her new home. They had obviously spent a lot of money— a long drive-in flanked by royal palms and beds of roses led up to the portico. There was apparently and even larger spread of lawns and flowerbeds in the rear of the house. I fired my first compliment at the house.

"What a beautiful frontage you have, Mrs Kumar!"

"Oh, thank you, thank you," she gushed, "but you have not seen my backside yet. It's much prettier than my front."

My second compliment, this time addressed to the hostess evoked an equally naive response. She was draped in a gossamer-thin sari through which one could see most of what she had. "And what a beautiful sari you are wearing!" I said.

"Oh this is very *maamooli*; I just wear it for streetwalking."

A young reader sends a South Indian version of how to spell Mississippi. First comes yumm. Then I come. Then my sissi. Then I peepee. Then I come again.

A busload of American tourists were heading towards Punjab on G.T. Road when suddenly the driver slammed the brakes.

Lying on the Road in front was a *Sardarjee* with his ear to the ground. Passengers trooped out of the bus and crowded around the man. "Hey, what are you doing down there pal?" asked one of the tourists.

The man slowly raised his head and replied: "Green Matador 25 km away travelling at 80 km."

"Wow," exclaimed the tourist, you can tell us that by listening to the road?"

"No," croaked the *Sardarjee*, "I fell off the damned thing."

Contributed by Mukhtiar Singh Bhatia, Jamshedpur

A group of Congress(I) MPs were comparing notes with one another. As usual their chief occupation was who was *nazdeek* (close) to the Prime Minister and who had been replaced by whom in the inner circles. Asked one of another who seemed to know the comings and goings on Race Course Road: "Have you seen the Prime Minister recently?"

Arre kahan! You ring and ring and no appointment is given. 'Too busy' is all that his secretaries say."

"But surely, you know him well enough to walk into the *kothi* without an appointment!"

"Those days are gone," replied the other sadly, "now its battalions outside and Italians inside."

Contributed by Satindra Singh

126

A minister of government whose knowledge of English was very poor was provided with a secretary to write speeches for him. "Give me a fifteen-minute speech on the non-aligned movement." ordered the boss.

The text was prepared to last exactly fifteen minutes. But when the minister proceeded to make his oration it took him half-an-hour to do so. The organisers of the conference were upset because their schedule went away. And the minister was upset because his secretary had let him down. He upbraided him: "I asked for a 15 minute speech; you gave me a half-hour speech. Why? he demanded.

"Sir, I gave a 15-minute speech. But you read out its carbon copy as well."

"There are going to be many major changes in the administration," opined a *sabjantawala*. Someone asked him, "If there are major changes, why not colonel changes?"

"You *bewakoof!* you don't know any English. Major means *wadda* (big) not a rank in the army."

"If major is *wadda*, then colonel is *wadda, wadda.*"

I do not know if you have heard this one as a commentary on the visit of the Chinese Foreign Minister, Huang Hua; but it is going round the social circles of Delhi.

Huang Hua aya, Huang Hua gaya. Kya hua?
"Thora hua ya bahut hua, kuch to hua!"

127

This one I picked up in London on my way back home. As the aircraft was taxying towards the runway to take off, the voice on the speaker welcomed passengers on board and introduced them to the pilot. "Your captain is Miss Mary Joystick...."

"You mean to tell me this plane is being piloted by a woman?" asked an alarmed passenger to a stewardess.

"Yes," sir, replied the stewardess. " So is the co-pilot, Miss Jane Understudy. So also are the radio operator and the navigator, they are all women in command."

"I must see this for myself", said the passenger. "Please take me to the cockpit."

"We don't call it that any more sir," replied the stewardess.

A deal was struck between an industrialist and a minister of government for the sanction of a licence for Rs 10 lakhs to be paid in cash. A note sanctioning the issue of licence was prepared and put up to the minister for his signatures. The industrialist, not being sure of the minister's intentions brought Rs five lakhs and handed them over to the minister's secretary— the remaining five to be paid on issue of licence. The file came back with the minister's remark: "Not accepted."

The industrialist promptly paid the remaining five lakhs and the file was taken back to the minister who simply added the letter E to the "not": "Note accepted."

We Indians are often accused of mutilating the English language. But, for real linguistic mayhem, the first prize must go to the Japanese. I collected quite a few samples based on their pronouncing the letter L as if it were an R. And vice versa. One favourite was a headline in a paper: "We play for General McArthur's erection." Another a hoarding sign: "Sunright soap - Lever Brothels Ltd." I have a few a few gems (should be Mikimoto pearls) from my friend P.N. Seth in Tokyo. The menu provides a few delectable items - like Humbug Steak, Poison au Gratin and Rogue Fart Cheese. The best is of a doctor who describes himself as a "Specialist for the decease of children" and prescribes "one tablet a day till passing away."

Regarding the benefits of abstinence, you may have heard the repartee between the abstainer General Montogomery and the gay liver, Winston Churchill. Says Monty: "I don't drink, I don't smoke and I am 100 per cent fit." Answers Winnie: "I smoke, I drink and I am 200 per cent fit."

My favourite is the one about an ageing rogue who wanted to live to be a hundred. "Give up smoking, drinking and going out with women," advised his doctor.

"And will I then be able to live up to one hundred years?" asked the rogue.

"I am not sure", replied the doctor "but it will certainly seem like it."

I never object to anyone calling me names or making fun of me. I believe in Burn's dictum to "see ourselves as others see us". Many of my readers see me as a name-dropper and a poseur. P.S. Ranganathan of New Delhi has parodied what he thinks I would have written on the deaths of Tagore, Marilyn Monroe and Karl Marx. The obit on the poet reads as follows:

"It was a rainy Sunday morning when I had the opportunity to meet the Nobel Prizewinner. Tagore was at a seaside resort in Switzerland, the charming landlocked country of Europe. I was just returning after a two-month holiday-cum-research tour of Polynesia, Hawaii and Las Vegas. I was working on a novel for my publishers, Tom, Dick and Harry, London. This novel was also to be published in America by Fung, Wag and Kneel Inc, New York."

"I had earlier phoned Tagore for an appointment. 'Sunday, 7.30. Will it suit you?' he asked in a clear voice. 'Oh anything will suit me except my suits stitched in India,' I said. There was hearty laughter at the other end of the phone. Surely, Tagore was a man with a high sense of humour!"

"When I went on the appointed day, I was slightly late- to be exact, by about 8 hours. Tagore received me at the porch and offered me *nimbu-de joiuce,* a delicious drink (certainly I did not expect the poet to offer me Scotch). For the next forty minutes we discussed the current literary trends. I was then vaguely planning a novel, later to be titled *A Train to Pakistan* (published by Hind Pocket Books or Orient Paperbacks or Pearl Publications. I don't exactly remember the name of the publisher, which is not quite material. The book is priced at Rs 4, which is quite material)."

"Tagore asked me what I was doing. 'Nothing of important I said," Oh, you Sardarjis are modest to a fault. With your remarkable talent, whatever you do will be important and will certainly make a great impact on the minds of intellectuals. Now, since we are alone, I can tell you this. Your writings are quite outstanding and you are sure to be awarded the Nobel Prize.'

"Tagore was a great soul with a great heart. He is gone. I only wish that his statement comes true." About Miss Monroe, the parody reads as follows:

"Marilyn had a soft corner for me. It was just by chance I was seated next to her in a Pan-Am jet from New York to London. 'Mr Khushwant, I presume, I am Marilyn Monroe, 'she introduced herself. 'Your name is familiar. But I am unable to place you,' I said hesitatingly. 'You must have seen a naked picture of a Hollywood actress in *Life*. It was mine,' she said. Then I remembered."

And Karl Marx:

"An outstanding thinker and a remarkable writer who was fascinated by my writings. In fact he told a common friend of ours—why should I withhold his name, he was Winston Churchill—well, Marx was telling Winston that he was keen to translate my novel into Russian. Winny—that was how I used to address him—later told me this when we met at Buckingham Palace for a party. I was thrilled by this piece of news but I had to politely decline the offer since another friend of mine was already at the job. If my readers would not say I am dropping names, I can say that the friend was no other person than Tolstoy. "This is what one 'K' can write about another 'K' in this moment of great anguish."

If this be the truth about me, it is time for me to take an overdose of barbiturates.

A Sardarji took his attractive sister to see the Taj Mahal. Some UP rustics sitting on the balcony overlooking the river Jamuna eyed the pair and one exclaimed loudly in his dialect: *"Yaar sardar kee joroo too bahut sunder hai* (Friends, the Sardar has a very pretty wife)." The Sardar took umbrage, came up to the fellow and ticked him of roundly. *"Abey saley! Joroo hogee teyree! Saadi to behen lagdee hai* (rascal! let her be your wife; she is my sister)."

Contributed by N.L. Gupta, Delhi

Q: Why are there no rains in northern India?
A: Because they have put *"Badal"* in Jail.

Contributed by J.P. Singh Kaka, N. Delhi

Dharmaraja, the divine Record Keeper summoned Yamdoot, the messenger of death and orderd: "Go down and get the atma of RamLal. His time is up."

Yamdoot went down and found Ram Lal. But however much he looked in Ram Lal's body, he could not find his *atma*. He reported back to Dharmaraj. "How can that be?" demanded the Record Keeper, "every person has to have a soul. Go and look more carefully."

Yamdoot went back and looked more carefully but failed to find Ram Lal's soul. Dharmraj consulted his records and could find no entry of a human being without an *atma*. "What does this fellow Ram Lal do for a living?" he asked.

"He is some kind of a minister in the government," replied Yamdoot.

"No wonder you couldn't find a soul in his body. Go back and look in his chair. That's where Indian politicians and ministers keep their *atmas*."

Urdudaans and *Angreziwalas* never stop making fun of the *Hindiwala's* by coining examples of ludicrous translations from their languages into Hindi. There is the well-known Hindi version of the A.I. Lawn Tennis Tournament as the *Akhil Bharatiya Gend-balla muth bher.* Professor Qadir of Mysore gave me two gems of translations of names of the poet Josh Malihabadi and Maulana Abul Kalam Azad. Josh dubbed as *Shair-i-Inqilab* (poet of the revolution) is Hindi-ised as *Uthal Puthal* (Revolution) *Kavi-ubal* (Josh) *Nav Puri* (Malihabadi). And Maulana Azad whose Arabic name *Abul Kalam* means father of speech has been Hindi-ised as *maha bakkoo chutera* (azad or free).

My tennis partner R.N. Palit of the Indian Police has put me a poser which I cannot answer. So I pass it on to my more erudite Hindi Bhasha readers. Palit asks why every Hindi noun, whether animate or inanimate has a gender? Furthermore, there seems no method or logic in the allocation of genders to inanimate nouns. Why, for instance, purely masculine appendages such as *moonch,* (moustache) and *daarhi* (beard) are feminine and the purely feminine append-age like *stan* (breast) masculine? The same applies to essentially masculine groups such as *sena, fauj,* police, *sarkar* (government) and *baraat* (bridegroom's party) all of which are made feminine gender.
Any ideas on the subject?

One day Gorbachev, Reagan and Rajiv Gandhi appeared before God to find out what was in store for their countries. Gorbachev asked: "When will my country be free from corruption?"

"Twenty-six years from now," replied God.

Reagan put him the same question. God replied: "It'll take time. At least another century."

"What about India?" asked Rajiv Gandhi.

God had tears in His eyes as He replied? "I won't live to seek the day when India will be free of corruption."

Contributed by Siddhantamangal Kashyap, Guwahati

A couple were celebrating the birth of their first child, a son. After the party was over, the husband spoke to his wife: "My dear, I have a very modern outlook on the size of a family. I think one son is good enough for us. So if you don't mind, I like to undergo a vasectomy. what do you think?"

"Do as you wish," replied the wife coyly. "You have your vasectomy now. I'll have my hysterectomy after I have had the third child."

A newly nominated Chief Minister — I beg his pardon, unanimously elected by his party—was under pressure from all his supporters to appoint them as Ministers of Cabinet. Or else!

The much harassed Chief Minister sought the advice of his guru. "Very simple", replied the sage, "select nine on three principles".

"O holy one!" pleaded the Chief Minister, "please enlighten this ignoramus on the three principles of selection".

"Three should be *sachha*—truthful."

The Chief Minister looked over the list of his supporters and crossed out all the names.

"Three should be *suchha*—clean."

The Chief Minister took a second look at the list and again crossed out all the names.

"Three should be *luchhas*—vagabonds."

The Chief Minister went over the list and looked more puzzled than before. "All of them qualify under the third category. What should I do?" he pleaded.

"Give all of them some kind of post or the other. Tell everyone that they are all *luchhas* and the only *sachha-suchha* person in the cabinet is the Chief Minister."

My friend Hukam Dev Yadav, MP from Bihar, stated in all solemnity in the Rajya Sabha that eucalyptus trees (which consume a lot of sub-soil water) had been introduced into India by foreign powers so that they would turn our fertile lands into deserts and we would have to import our foodgrains from them. This is on a level with the explanation of the poor performance of our hockey team at the Los Angeles Olympic games: It was the foreign hand.

135

A girl was given in marriage to a young man who had four brothers living in the same house. During the day the men were out working in the fields. They returned home after dusk for their evening meal when their mother and the brother's new wife served them with their faces dutifully veiled. After a fortnight the young wife demurely asked her mother-in-law. "Beybey, please tell me which one of your four sons is my husband?"

The mother-in-law replied: "Bahurani, you've only been here 15 days; I lived 25 years with my husband and his brothers and never got to know which one he was."

Contributed by Shivtar Singh Dalla, Ludhiana

The opening Indian batsmen in a Test match against the West Indies were Sunil Gavaskar and a new find, Sardar Stroke Singh. Marshall, the pace bowler, opened the bowling for his side. The first ball went sizzling past the off-stump to be collected by the wicketkeeper. Sardar Stroke Singh did not as much as budge from his place. Marshall bowled his second, third and fourth balls all about the wicket with Stroke Singh standing still as a statue. The fifth delivery was declared "No ball" by the umpire. Like a true Test professional Sardar Stroke Singh went tapping the pitch midway towards Sunil Gavaskar and said, "I knew from the very begining the fellow did not have a ball in his hand."

Contributed by Dr A. Sahuk, New Delhi

Two donkeys met at a wayside and got talking. One was a robust looking fellow who was without a master; the other a miserable looking specimen who belonged to brick-kiln owner. The robust fellow hee-hawed: "What's the matter with you? You look famished and woebegone."

"My master is very cruel. He gives me very little to eat, loads me with hundreds of bricks and beats me with his stick."

"So! why don't you run away and like me live off the fat of the land?"

The lean-thin donkey explained, "You see my master has a very pretty daughter. He also beats and abuses her."

"What's that to do with you?"

"Every time he thrashes the girl he says. "One of these days I'll marry you off to this donkey. My job has better prospects."

An English teacher examining students of his class asked a boy named Surya Prakash his name in English. "Sir, my name is Sunlight," replied the boy.

"And what is your name?" the teacher asked another boy named Jeewan Nath.

"Sir, my name is Life Buoy".

The third boy named Akash Deep when asked the same question answered, "I am Skylamp".

The teacher turned to the fourth boy and asked, "What is your father's name?"

The boy whose father's name was Prabhu Dayal, replied, "Sir, his name is God-is-kind."

Contributed by Shivtar Singh Dalla, Ludhiana

A Punjabi with more money than sense had a more-than-necessary fecund wife who bore him a child every year with unfailing regularity. Having had more offsprings, than he wanted to share his wealth, he consulted the doctor of a family planning clinic. He tried all the child-preventive gadgetry but nothing would stop the ·wife from presenting him with yet another child. Ultimately the Punjabi gentleman decided to go to the United States to consult the best doctors in the world. He found the most renowned family planning specialist and spelled out his problem. "Well, Mr. Punjabi," drawled the Yankee medico, "if you've tried all those preventives and they have failed, the best I can suggest is that you keep away from your wife."

"But doctor," protested the Punjabi, "I've tried that too."

An argument arose as to which State Government excelled in corruption. The following story settled the issue.

Six years ago an MLA from Kerala visited Chandigarh and called on a Punjab Minister at his house. He was amazed at the ostentation and asked his old friend "How did you manage to acquire so much wealth?"

"Are you really interested to know?."

"Of course, yes. A little extra knowledge always helps."

"Then wait till tomorrow, and I shall explain fully."

The next day the Minister drove the MLA down the highway for several kilometers in his personal Honda.

He stopped the car, both of them got out and the Minister pointed his finger to a spot down the beautiful valley.

"Do you see the big bridge over there ?" he asked.

"Yes," replied the MLA.

"Half the cost of the bridge went into my pocket."

Four years later the Punjabi who in the meantime lost his Ministership, went on a holiday to Trivandrum and called on his old friend, who in the meanwhile had become a Minister. "By God", said the Punjabi, "you have beaten me flat. Crystal chandeliers, Italian marble, Mercedes. Tell me how you managed it."

"I will tell you tomorrow," said the Minister. Next day the Minister drove him down the highway, stopped the car at a spot overlooking a valley and the Minister pointed his finger to a spot down the valley, and asked.

"Do you see the bridge over there?"

"I see no bridge," said the Punjabi.

"Quite right," said the Minister. "The entire cost of the bridge went into my pocket."

Contributed by K.S. Menon, Bombay

139

A reader who wishes to remain anonymous has compared Rajiv Gandhi's pre-election foray to West Bengal as a quixotic assault on the citadel of Marxism. What remains to be determined are the identities of his Sancho Panza and the donkey he rode on.

He proceeds to elaborate by comparing today's Delhi durbar to that of Shah Alam's whose "empire" extended from the Red Fort to village Palam, eight kilometres away. Two men who had a dispute approached the Emperor to settle their quarrel. "Your Majesty, we are your loyal subjects living across the Jumna within a stone's throw from your exalted Fort (Qila-e-Moalla). Please be our arbitrator."

"The other side of the Jumna, did you say?" demanded the Emperor.

"Yes, your Majesty."

"Take your dispute elsewhere. Our writ no longer runs beyond the river."

Three Inspector Generals of Police belonging to the USA, the USSR and India happened to travel together on an international flight. They exchanged notes regarding the efficiency and quickness of their respective police forces. The Russian IG claimed that they submit a report of a crime to their Home department within fourteen days. The American IG went a step ahead and boasted that they did so within fourteen hours. The Indian IG of police who was listening to these tall claims with rapt attention gave a mysterious smile and said that they did things more efficently in India. When questioned by his co passengers he replied "Our police in fact know a good fourteen days in advance about the nature, time and place of crime that is yet to take place."

Contributed by Dr K.K. Chibber, N. Delhi

A Punjabi peasant on his first flight to take up a job in England got a seat on a British airline. Came lunch time and the stewardess brought a tray of European savouries. "No", said the peasant firmly as he undid a small bundle and took out a *makki ki roti*. "What is this you are munching? asked the stewardess.

"This bread India," he replied.

A little while later, the stewardess brought a trayful of puddings of different kinds. Once again the peasant shook his head as he produced a lump of *gur* from his pocket and put it in his mouth.

"What is this you are chewing?" asked the stewardess.

"This sweet India," he replied.

When the stewardess came to take away the lunch trays, the peasant let out a loud belch.

"And what is this?" demanded the stewardess sternly.

"This is Air India."

Contributed by Vijay Dawar, Faridabad

Question: "What is the difference between a Congress politician and a dacoit?"

Answer: "A dacoit robs first and then goes to jail; a Congress politician goes to jail first and then commits robbery."

Contributed by U.S. Mani, Paonta Sahib

Two Punjabi farmers ploughing their fields saw Mig-23 fly overhead at great speed emitting a lot of smoke from its tail. One remarked "Bantia, look how fast it is going and the racket it is making!"

"Sure, replied the other, "if somebody set fire to your tail, you would run faster than the plane and fart much louder."

Mr and Mrs Punjabi had an Anglo-Indian couple move into the neighbouring apartment. Mrs Punjabi noticed that every morning the neighbours kissed each other and mumbled some words. Unable to contain herself Mrs Punjabi asked new neighbour, *"Kee kahindee hain khasam noo roj savery* (what is it you say to your husband first thing in the morning)?" The lady replied, "We say good morning. *Jiska meaning hai, achha subah"*.

Mrs Punjabi was impressed. The next morning she greeted her husband: *"Godda marnee* (I'll stick my knee in your groin)."

Mr Punjabi promptly replied: *"Toon godda maarni* (if you kick me in my groin), *main tainee lat maarni* (I'll kick you—on the arse)."

Contributed by Natrajan Anand, Howrah

Three Russian officials found themselves in jail. A Press reporter was allowed to interview them. He asked the first man, "Why were you sent to prison?"

"I was late coming to the office, so the boss ordered me to be sent to jail."

When asked the same, the second person replied. "I went to the office before the scheduled time. The boss thought I was spying for a foreign country, so he had me locked up."

The third prisoner on having the question repeated, replied: "I arrived at the office on the dot. The boss ordered my arrest on the grounds that if I was punctual to the minute I must own an imported and not a Russian watch."

Contributed by Baghel Bajwa. Village Barnala

Three friends, a Hindu, a Muslim and a Sikh, all great admirers of Bir Bajrang Bali were hotly arguing about what community Hanumanji belonged to. The Hindu was outraged by their claims: "How could Hanuman possibly be Muslim?" he demanded of his Muslim friend. "We have *Ahsan, Rehman, Sulaiman* and many other Muslim names ending with *aan*. Hanuman could well have been one such name."

"And you Sardarji," said the Hindu aggressively. "Sikhism came into being a thousand years after the Ramayana. How can you say Hanuman was Sikh?"

"Quite clearly Hanuman was Sikh," replied the Sardarji. "Here we have someone who does not know the person whose wife has been abducted, he does not know the lady who has been abducted, and he has no enmity towards the abductor. Nevertheless he sets his tail on fire and burns up a whole city. Who else would do such a thing except a Sardarji!"

Contributed by Harjeet Kaur

Another pressman asked a politician: "Sir, what are your views on the independent state of Pakistan? "The politician replied, "Our forefathers laid down their lives to achieve freedom."

"And sir where have you spent most of your life since Pakistan became free?"

"In Kot Lakhpat." (Kot Lakhpat is known for its jail)

Girl friend in Tokyo writes: "Dear Harry, you are gone six months and I am six months gone. Shall I carry Harry or commit hara-kiri?" The Japanese tale proves the adage: "The road to hell is paved with faulty contraception."

143

This one I heard during my days at the Bar. Before the case was taken up the two lawyers engaged by the opposing sides decided to cut the other to size. "I am told you are an absolute fraud, a 420. Today I am going to expose the truth about you."

"And I happen to know that you are the world's biggest liar, wait till I strip you of all your false pretensions."

The magistrate intervened and said "Evidently you gentlemen need no introduction as you seem to know. each other well. Now we can get on with the case."

Seen inside a DTC bus:

Aana free
Jaana free
Pakray gaye to
Khana free

Contributed by J.P. Singh Kaka, N.Delhi

A very agitated youngman barged into a Family Planning clinic and angrily spoke to the doctor: "You perfomed that vasectomy operation on me, but my wife is pregnant again. You obviously don't know your job."

"Calm down. It is you I operated on, not your neighbours."

There's lots to a name if it is Indian. Some even grade the amount of religious learning a person has acquired. Knowing only one *Veda* does not entitle you to an honorific, but if you know two, you can be a Dwivedi, if three, a Trivedi, and if you know all the four, a Chaturvedi.

It is said that a Hindi writer named Trivedi went to complain to the Editor of a paper who had published his story but given the name of the author as Dwivedi.

"*Sampadakji*, I have to thank you for publishing my story," he said, "but why did you have to reduce my rank from a Trivedi to Dwivedi?"

The *Sampadakji* apologised and promised to make amends. "The next two strories I publish by you, I will name you Chaturvedi and make up your loss."

The recent Allahabad by-election evoked the following one-line comments in the event of the Congress-I with its open-palm symbol winning: "*haath kee safaee*"—sleight of hand.

And an apter comment on the outcome—"*haath ka safaaya*"—the hand wiped out.

Contributed by J.P. Singh Kaka, New Delhi

The style of living of some of our ruling party Ministers has produced a crop of jokes. The Chief Minister of a *ghareebee hatao* State who had risen from rags to riches was very irked by stories against him circulating in the State and ordered his Commissionerrof Police to bring the author of anti-C.M. jokes to him. The joke-maker was nabbed and brought to the C.M's mansion. He began looking round the well-furnished drawing room with chandeliers,plush sofas and Persian carpets.

"What are you looking for?" demanded the C.M. angrily.

"I was simply looking around to see how well you live," replied the joke-maker.

"What of it" demanded the C.M. "With our *bees sootri*—20 point-programme, in 20 years everyone will be living like this."

"I didn't make that joke," replied the joke-maker. "It is absolutely new."

Two Congress party leaders were taking a walk in a park when they saw a hundred rupee note on the ground. Both grabbed it and began quarrelling over who should keep it.

"Lets stop arguing," suggested one "and put it in the party fund."

The other paused and replied, "There is no point in making it do the usual rounds. Lets go fity-fifty right now."

Adivasis of a district approached their Member of Parliament and said, "Our *Pradhan Mantri* has visited every part of the country but has never been to see us. You are our representative, you must get him to visit us here."

The MP demurred. He was a member of the Opposition and was hardly expected to invite the Prime Minister. But the Adivasis insisted that he get the *Pradhan Mantri* somehow or the other. Then the wily MP thought of a way out: "You see, the Prime Minister likes to dress in the costumes of the people he visits. Most of you go naked. So even if he agrees to come here, what should I tell him about what he should wear."

Contributed by Krishna Goel, Ladwa

Rajiv Gandhi, Hinduja and Amitabh decided to become partners and make a film. Hinduja said: "I will put up the money for the film!"

Amitabh said: "I will act in the film!"

Both of them then turned to Rajiv and asked: "What will you do for the film?"

Rajiv said: "*Hum dekhenge....*"

Question: Why is the Indian Government the most neutral in the world?

Answer: Because it does not even interfere in its own affairs.

A Sardarji got into a crowded bus and forcibly sat into somebody's seat saying, "I am a lion's son". The poor fellow had no other alternative than to cover the distance standing all along. After some time when the Sardarji got down at his destination this fellow took out his head out of the window and asked "Sardarji, did your mother go to the jungle or did the lion come to your house?"

Contributed by Dr. J.P. Singh, Haryana

A youngster was very impressed after spending a lot of time with Burton's volumes of the *Arabian Nights*. One day he confessed to his intimate friend, "How I wish I had a harem as some of the Sultans are reported to have had!" His friend was a calmer and more reflective type, said he, "Oh! I do not know. Have you ever thought of all the mother-in-law's who will be in tow?"

Contributed by Wg. Cdr. S. Sankara Narayanan, Madras

A lady sued a man for abusing her in a filthy language in public. During arguments the defence counsel asked her to state in the court exactly what the accused said.

The lady replied that it was so filthy, that no decent person would like to hear that.

The counsel said, "Then please step up and whisper it to his lordship."

Contributed by R.P.D. Sud, Ludhiana

An elderly Sardarji was boasting of his knowledge of development of science and technology in India. "My first son", he said "When he married, in the late seventies we took 'Black & White' photographs of his wedding."

"And when my second son got married, we could take coloured photographs of his wedding. That was in the early eighties" he continued.

"And my third child, my daughter, who got married recently, I gave her a video cassette of her marriage to see."

"And what do you think shall be the development when you marry your next child after a couple of years" the other person asked.

The Sardarji pondered for a moment "I shall get it programmed on a Personalised Computer" he said.

Contributed by Rajesh P. Shirodkar, Bombay

The harried clerk suffering from insomnia never got to sleep before dawn; then slept right through the alarm and so never made it to the office on time. Upon being reprimanded by his boss, he decided to consult a doctor. The doctor gave him some sleeping pills. That night he fell asleep immediately and experienced a pleasant rest. In the morning he awoke before the alarm rang, jumped out of the bed with new verve and vigour. When he arrived at his office promptly, he told his boss, "Those pills I got from my doctor really work. I had no trouble at all waking up this morning."

"That's nice," the boss replied, "But where were you yesterday?"

Contributed by R. Ravi, Bangalore

A Congress Minister's son was doing very badly in college. The father was very worried and wrote to the Principal seeking his advice about the future prospects of his son. The Principal wrote back to the Minister: "Dear Sir, I have had your son put through a vocational aptitude test. Our results show that he is best suited for a job in your Ministry."

"And that's not all, I even get chance to fly an aeroplane" the Bengali boasted. Sardarji did not like the attitude of the Bengali. "I will learn to fly a helicopter within a week and show you" the Sardarji declared.

And indeed the Sardarji had decided to learn flying a helicopter. After a week he called the Bengali to see his new talent.

He sat in the helicopter and began to fly it. The helicopter went up into the sky. The crowd cheered and praised the Sardarji.

Suddenly the helicopter came down and crashed. Fortunately the Sardarji was not hurt.

"What happened?" the Bengali asked.

"As I went up 100 metres, I started feeling cold. But I went higher. I started feeling more cold. As I went higher and higher, I started feeling more and more cold. So I switched off the big fan which is above the helicopter" the Sardarji answered.

Contributed by Rajesh P. Shirodkar, Bombay

The large, burly man approached the bartender and said, "I see by the sign of your window that you're looking for a bouncer, has the post been filled?"

"Not yet", said the bartender. "Have you had any experience?"

'No", the man replied, "but watch this!" He walked over to a loud-mouthed drunkard at the back of the room, lifted him off his feet and threw him sprawling into the street. Then having returned to the bar he said, "How's that?"

"Great!" admitted the bartender. "But you'll have to ask the boss about the job. I only work here"

"Fine" said the burly man, "Where is he?"

"Just coming back in from the front door".

Contributed by R. Ravi, Bangalore

A man had four beautiful daughters in the age group of 17 to 20. The prospective son-in-law was told that he could select any one of the four. The eldest one was a telephone operator. The next one was a bank officer, the third a doctor, and the youngest a teacher. The boy selected the youngest and married her.

His friends asked him later why he preferred the youngest daughter when he had better options.

He replied, "The telephone operator is in the habit of saying 'Wait please'; The bank officer of saying 'Stand in the queue'; Doctor will say 'Relax and take it lightly'; But the school teacher will always say 'Repeat, repeat...'."

Contributed by J.P. Singh, Haryana

We Indians are often called a litigious lot and many of us despair on the practice of our labyrinthine legal system. But perhaps many of us are not aware that American lawyers are no less mercenary than their Indian brethren and some of the legal judgements handed down by US Courts will amaze us.

For example, in 1984, an American woman under the influence of drink drove her Porsche car at 60 mph in a 25 mph zone and killed a man. Result? Porsche was asked by a US Court to pay $ 2.5 million in damages for having designed a car deemed too high in performance for an average driver.

Another example, while attempting to burgle a school a burglar fell through the skylight. The company that insured the school was asked to pay $ 260,000 in damages and give the would-be burglar $ 1500 per month for life.

The joke goes that Americans can be divided into three broad groups and each group deals with its enemies in its own way. Americans belonging to the first group sue their enemy. Those belonging to the second group shoot their enemy. And those belonging to the third group shoot their enemy and then sue his widow for mental anguish brought about by guilt and imprisonment !

Contributed by Debashish Bose, Calcutta

A car was involved in an accident in a street. As expected a large crowd collected. A newspaper reporter anxious to get his story could not get near the car. But being a bright young fellow, he started crying loudly, "Let me through! Let me through! I am the son of the victim."

The crowd made way for him. Lying in front of the damaged car was the donkey it had run over.

Contributed by Vineet Khanna, Chandigarh

"I understand you had an argument with your wife?"

"Yes."

"How did it end up?"

"Ultimately she came down on her knees", and said "If you are a man, come out from beneath the bed and fight like a man!"

Contributed by R.P.D. Sud, Ludhiana

A senior official of a ministry decided to spend a whole day in one of the departments under him. He got there before the office opened and noted that many of the staff came in half an hour or an hour after opening time. He sent for the Superintendent and told him to warn the staff that anyone coming late in the future would be penalised. In the evening he saw many clerks leaving office early. He again sent for the Superintendent and rebuked him: "What is going on in your office? So many clerks come late and leave early!"

"Sir, they don't want to be late twice on the same day," replied the Superintendent.

Contributed by Dr. D.K. Saxena, Jaipur

A man was sitting in a train, slowly shaking his head from one side to another like a pendulum. Finally the man sitting opposite to him asked him why he was doing so?

The man replied, "So I can tell the time."

"Well, what is the time?"

"Eight-thirty," said the man still shaking his head.

"You are wrong. It's quarter to eight."

"Oh! then, I must be slow;" the man answered, speeding up.

Contributed by Praveen Nepalia, Rajasthan

It was a summer night. Mr. and Mrs. Rao were having dinner. Suddenly there was power failure. Mrs. Rao lit a candle and they continuted with their dinner Mr. Rao finished his meal and saw his wife perspiring. He got up. She looked at him enquiringly.

"I will switch on the fan dear!" he said.

"What! you want me to eat in the dark?" she cried.

"Why?" he asked.

"Don't you have any commonsense? If you switch on the fan won't it blow out the candle?" she retorted.

Contributed by K. Virabhadra Sastri, Vijayawada

A leader of the Opposition party was soliciting votes at an election meeting. "Brothers, this time you should vote for my party. The ruling party has cheated you for many years. Now give me a chance."

Contributed by Shashank Shekhar, Meerut

A new word borrowed from Hindi and used freely in all languages in India among the workers of factories and other labour organisations is "*gherao*". It is an action taken by the striking workers to dissuade the non-participants in the strike from going about their normal duties and in effect to earn their active sympathy to the strike. The process may be non-violent to start with, but there is no knowing where it may end. The word came into use during the first half of the sixties. Hindustan Aeronautics Limited, Nasik was formed in 1964; and to begin with a large contingent of the staff was selected to man it from the parent organisation, Hindustan Aeronautics Limited, Bangalore. The migrants hastened to assure me that "*gherao*" was not one more 'Rao' from Bangalore.

Contributed by Wg. Cdr. S. Sankara Narayanan, Madras

A Sardarji asked his son, "What is 9 multiplied by 8?" The boy replied, "74".

Sardarji patted the boy and took out a piece of chocolate and gave it to him.

On seeing this his neighbour said, "9 multiplied by 8 is equal to 72, and not 74 as the boy said."

Sardarji replied, "He is improving, yesterday he was saying it is 88."

Contributed by Dr. J.P. Singh, Haryana

Lahore's Gulbarg colony where retired government servants have built themselves large bungalows is popularly known as *Rishwatpura*—graft town. This story is of a humble excise inspector who on the completion of his larger-than-legitimate mansion had inserted near the entrance a marble slab with the Koranic inscription *Huza bin fazl-i-Rabbi*—this by the grace of God. (A very common practice amongst Muslims). One morning as the house-owner strolled out of the lawn towards the entrance he saw a man gazing at his mansion, praising its grandeur with *wah wahs* and *kya khoobs!* but also shedding copious tears. The mansion owner approached him and asked: "Janaab, I do not understand why if you like my humble *ghareeb khana* you are also crying over it. Is there something that does not please you?

"I think your *daulat khana* is wonderful. What makes me cry is that you should give credit for it to the wrong person," he replied pointing to the marble slab. "It is not God who taught you how to make money as an excise inspector but I. You should have given me the credit."

"And who may you be, Sir?" asked the irate mansion-owner. "I am Satan".

The Home Minister sent a registered letter to the Akali leaders ensconced in the Yatri Niwas of the Golden Temple: "Hand over the culprit at once", it demanded.

Promptly came back the reply from Jarnail Singh Bhindranwale: "We have a Harpreet Singh and Gurpreet Singh and a Jaspreet Singh but we have no Kulpreet Singh."

This one is from my college days in India 25 years ago. A new out-patient's department block was built at the medical college and a minister invited to inaugurate it. The dean took the minister round the various rooms explaining what they were. "And this, sir, is the new radiology department."

The *mantri-mahoday* turned to his PA. "Our radio at home has been giving us trouble. Have it sent here to put it right."

Contributed by Dr. Suresh Pathak, Ruinford (England)

Wife : How have you managed to get home so early today?

Husband: My boss lost his temper with me and shouted. "Go to hell." So I came home.

Contributed by J.P. Singh Kaka, New Delhi

A man lost his brand new bicycle and lodged a complaint at the police station. "Please give particulars of the bicycle," ordered the inspector.

"Hero, brand new, black frame, black saddle, black carrier, silver bell...."

"That description would fit every new bicycle," interrupted the official. "Tell me something special about your machine."

After thinking over the problem for a moment, the man replied, *"Thanedar Sahib,* every time a lady's cycle is parked alongside it, it's bell begins to ring."

Contributed by A.P. Singh, Chandigarh

The *mundoo* (boy servant) came crying to his master, *"Sahib, Bibiji* slapped me on the face."

"So what?" assured the master, "have you ever seen me crying?"

Sundarji, Sundarji:

Sundarji, Sundarji, what have you done?

"I've bloody well added more fuel to fire in the Bofors gun."

Sundarji, Sundarji, was it not very unkind?

"Dammit! They didn't make me Ambassador, so I kicked their behind."

Contributed by R.E. Canteenwala

"No Trespass."

A signboard in Hindi above the entrance of a house read: "*Andar mat aao* —do not enter."

Somebody put the *matra oo* under the letter 'M' of the second word. You work that out.

A judge, irritated by a lawyer's behaviour, admonished him, "You are crossing the limits."

"*Kaun saala aisa kehta hai,*" roared the lawyer.

"How dare you call me *saala* —brother-in-law? I'll have you charged for 'contempt of court'," said the judge angrily.

"My Lord misunderstood me," replied the lawyer coolly, "I do not call you *saala*, all I said was *kaun sa law aisa kahta hai* —which law says so?"

Contributed by J.P. Singh Kaka, New Delhi

Dear Reader,

Welcome to the world of **Orient Paperbacks**—India's largest selling paperbacks in English. We hope you have enjoyed reading this book and would want to know more about **Orient Paperbacks.**

There are more than 400 **Orient Paperbacks** on a variety of subjects to entertain and inform you. The list of authors published in **Orient Paperbacks** includes, amongst others, distinguished and well-known names as Dr. S. Radhakrishnan, R.K. Narayan, Raja Rao, Manohar Malgonkar, Khushwant Singh, Anita Desai, Kamala Das, Dr. O.P. Jaggi, Norman Vincent Peale, Sasthi Brata and Dr. Promilla Kapur. **Orient Paperbacks** truly represent the best of Indian writing in English today.

We would be happy to keep you continuously informed of the new titles and programmes of **Orient Paperbacks** through our monthly newsletter, **Orient Literary Review.** Send in your name and full address to us today. We will start sending you **Orient Literary Review** completely free of cost.

Available at all bookshops or by VPP

ORIENT PAPERBACKS
Madarsa Road, Kashmere Gate
Delhi-110 006